ANALYSIS MATTERS

A Study Guide to London Examinations'
Advanced Level Musical History and Analysis Papers

Chronological Group 2 of
the London Anthology of Music

1st Edition
by David Bowman

Rhinegold Publishing Limited
241 Shaftesbury Avenue
London WC2H 8EH
Telephone : 0171 333 1721
Fax : 0171 333 1769

First Published June 1998 in Great Britain

Rhinegold Publishing Limited
241 Shaftesbury Avenue
London WC2H 8EH
Telephone : 0171 333 1721
Fax : 0171 333 1769

Analysis Matters, Chronological Group 2
British Library Cataloguing in Publication Data.
A catalogue record for this book is available from the British Library

ISBN 0 946890 78 1

Printed in Great Britain by Perfectaprint, Byfleet, Surrey

To Jill

Preface

In response to requests from teachers this new edition of *Analysis Matters* has been published before two-year courses in Musical History and Analysis begin in September 1998. It is intended that courses for Paper 4 should be based upon Chronological Group II in the *London Anthology of Music* (LAM). These 30 examples of music from the late Renaissance to the late 20th century will constitute the material upon which history and analysis questions will be set in the years 2000 and 2001.

Previous editions of *Analysis Matters* have been intended as revision guides for the use of students in the last term of the course. Consequently the notes on each item have been particularly concise. The emphasis in this new edition is somewhat different. It is still intended for students rather than teachers, and it is still intended that the book should supplement rather than supplant the work of teachers. It is recognised, however, that the notes are now likely to be used piecemeal as the course progresses. This being so an overview of all 30 items cannot be assumed. Consequently the notes on each item are more comprehensive than those provided in previous editions.

The Guide is in two parts. Part I consists of notes on each of the 30 items in Chronological Group II. Part II, a glossary printed on lavender-coloured paper, is intended to be detached so that it can be used to check the meaning of the technical vocabulary used in Part I. The glossary is not a dictionary. Only those terms used in Part I which might need to be explained to students at this level are included. Technical vocabulary is also used without explanation in the Glossary, but unfamiliar terms used under one heading will be found under another heading elsewhere in the Glossary.

It can not be too strongly emphasised that analysis should be based on the sound of music. Before work begins on each item the music should be played often enough for an internalised image of it to be accessible from the printed notation in the *Anthology*. Only then should these notes be consulted.

The syllabus and the examination lay great stress upon understanding as opposed to rote learning. It is therefore suggested that the Glossary should be used as a means of ensuring that analytical concepts have been understood. Dictionary definitions of musical terms can often seem baffling, but confusion can turn to enlightenment once a concrete example has been heard. Every one of the entries in the Glossary is illustrated with at least one example from the scores in Chronological Group II (or, where necessary, to other music in the *Anthology*). It is strongly recommended that these references be followed up diligently. It should be remembered that, even if a precise technical term can not be remembered in the examination, the use of a phrase or sentence which accurately paraphrases the term will be accepted by the examiners. This thought should be a comfort when confronted with the extensive list of terms contained in the Glossary.

Boltby, May 1998

David Bowman has for sixteen years been Chief Examiner for the University of London's Advanced Level music syllabuses. His prior publications include the *London Anthology of Music*, the award-winning *Sound Matters* co-authored with Bruce Cole, and *Aural Matters* with Paul Terry. David has been a regular contributor to *Music Teacher* since 1990. He teaches at Ampleforth College.

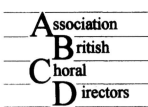

LAM 2

Gabrieli: Ricercare del 12º Tono (1586)

Title and form: The ricercare began life as an instrumental transcription of the 16th century motet (eg LAM 1) and, even when it became an independent original instrumental composition, it was still contrapuntal in texture and sometimes modal. The title means "to search out", the idea being to "research" all possible ways of treating a motive or motives in a contrapuntal texture. In the 17th century the ricercare developed into the baroque fugue (eg LAM 35b).

The canzona began life as an instrumental transcription of the 16th century French chanson. Like the chanson it was lighter in style, less modal, and included dance-like rhythms. It fell into a number of sections, some of them homophonic and some of them repeated. In the 17th century the sections of the canzona became the movements of the baroque sonata (eg LAM 14).

LAM 2 is a canzona in all but name. It is based on a couple of motives treated contrapuntally, but the style is light and only fleetingly modal. The extract shows just the first two sections (A and B) and the beginning of a contrasting section in triple time (C) of a structure which can be represented as ABCDCDA, ie seven sections, the last three being repeats of previous sections.

The remainder of the title (*del duodècimo tono*) means that the music was written in the 12th tone. For all practical purposes this is exactly the same as a major scale.

Rhythm: The long-short-short-long rhythm of the chanson is evident at the start of the second section. Throughout, the rhythms are dance-like, they emphasise the simple quadruple metre and include obvious syncopations, usually as the music approaches a cadence (eg the uppermost part in the second half of bar 25).

Melody: Repeated notes (another feature of the chanson), triadic figures and conjunct movement in C major with occasional modal touches (the uppermost part in bar 10 sounds to modern ears as though it needs an F♯, while the B♭s in bars 23 and 25 suggest the Mixolydian mode).

Harmony: Apart from suspensions (most obviously at cadences) the harmony is consonant and uses only root position and first inversion triads (the former predominating). The cadences always sound major, eg V$^{4-3}$ and I in C major in bars 13-14, and the same progression in G major at the end of the extract. At other points the progressions can sound modal, eg the root position triads a step apart in bars 17-18 (I-II-I in C major), and the B♭ major triads on the flattened 7th of C major in bars 23 and 25.

Texture: Although printed on two staves the music is in four real parts throughout (the only point at which this is not entirely clear is bar 3 where the "alto" part moves from the treble to the bass clef on the third beat). It can be played on any combination of instruments which were available in the late 16th century (eg four viols or cornetti and trombones). The first section is imitative, each entry beginning with the same motive of four quavers and four crotchets but modified thereafter (eg the stepwise quavers in the alto part of bar 2 become leaping quavers in the bass of bar 3, one of the notes heard in the alto is omitted in the bass and the alto's minim D becomes a crotchet B in the bass' imitation). In bars 9-12 the entries of the parts are telescoped. This stretto is particularly obvious in bar 11 where bass, alto, soprano and tenor enter one after the other on every beat of the bar.

The second section is more varied in texture. It begins with an antiphonal effect and there are canzona-like passages of homophony (eg bars 21³-23).

Style and genre: Late renaissance ensemble canzona.

Historical context: Andrea Gabrieli was born in Venice but became a close friend of Lassus (LAM 1) when he went to work under him at the Bavarian court in Munich. He was the first native composer to gain the position of Director of Music at St. Mark's in Venice where he composed much polychoral music for the splendidly colourful and extravagant services. He was Giovanni Gabrieli's uncle and the effect of their polychoral style may be judged by the younger man's motet *In ecclesiis* (LAM 10). It is likely that this Ricercare/canzona would have been performed on brass instruments in St. Mark's, perhaps as one of the great processions made its way from the piazza doors to the sanctuary.

LAM 4

Morley: Phillis, I faine wold die now (1595)

Title and text: A Dialogue to 7 voices = a musical conversation for 7 voices, three of them forming a choir (quier) of high voices representing the young shepherdess, Phillis, the others forming a four-voice choir of low voices representing the young shepherd, Amintas. These two characters are drawn from *L'Aminto*, a pastoral by the 18th century Italian poet Tasso, in which Amintas pursues Phillis in the blissful setting of Arcadia. The poem hinges on a conceit regarding the word *die* which could mean a sexual climax as well as its more normal meaning. Hence the minor-mode suspensions and chromaticisms that occur when Amintas pleads for mercy are really mock-tragic. The same conceit occurs in many madrigal texts of the period, including the Italian text for LAM 6 by Guarini (who also wrote a pastoral about Amintas). The two choirs are kept apart as the lovers flirt and argue, but they come together in the concluding massive seven-voice homophony when they agree that *time and love ... will provide for this our anguish.*

Rhythm: In homophonic passages verbal accents coincide with metrical accents on long notes (eg *I love thee* in bars 11-12) thus highlighting the most important words (in this case Phillis' tantalising admission of love). In imitative passages the individual melodic lines are more independent of the overall metre so that verbal accents do not always coincide with strong beats, eg *This unawares doth daunt me* on page 10 in which the two most important verbal stresses (*-wares* and *daunt*) are sung on strong beats by the second soprano but on weak beats by the other two voices. Syncopation often occurs at cadence points, eg bar 46 where the accented syllable *lea* is articulated off the beat in the upper two voices. It can also occur as a deliberate effect, eg bar 45 where the accented syllable *fit* is articulated off the beat in all voices. This dance-like effect is obviously deliberate: it suggests the fun that may be had when the two lovers have more time to devote to each other. Generally speaking the flirtatious Phillis is represented by faster note values than the supplicant Amintas, whose mock-gravity is reflected in longer note values. Only when agreement is reached do both choirs sing homorhythmically.

Melody: Predominantly conjunct. A leap is usually followed by stepwise movement, often with the melodic line returning within the leap. The real bass part is more angular than the other voices because it serves as the foundation for tonal harmonies (this is specially true at the frequent perfect cadences where the real bass is obliged to leap down a fifth or up a fourth (see Example 4). There are some exceptions to these generalisations, eg the point of imitation in the last system of page 12 of the *Anthology* is based on a figure of two consecutive falling thirds. The melodies are nominally in the Dorian mode transposed to G, but frequent sharpening of the 7th degree (F♯) and flattening of the 6th degree (E♭) give the music a feeling of G minor (see Example 4, bars 26-28).

Harmony: All the chords are root position or first inversion triads built on a scale which, with chromatic alterations to the Dorian mode transposed to G, gives the following possible notes for composition: G, A, B♭, C, D, E♭ (a chromatic alteration of the sixth degree of the mode), E♮, F♮ and F♯ (another chromatic alteration). The only other chromatic alteration to the mode is a sharpened third (tierce de Picardie) in the tonic triad at the frequent perfect cadences. When this G major chord is followed by a G minor triad at the start of the next phrase this frequently causes false relations. These features can be found in bar 28 of Example 4 where the tierce de Picardie (B♮) is immediately contradicted by a B♭ in the G minor triad of Phillis' choir (the arrow heads show the two notes of the false relation). Only twice does Morley use this sharpening of the third degree of the scale other than as a tierce de Picardie. In both instances they induce a brief C minor colouring to the tonality (bars 5 and 38 in the bass part).

The only true dissonances (2nds, 4ths and 7ths from the bass) are suspensions. These are shown by the figuring below Example 4. In bar 25 the dissonant tied middle C forms a 4th with the bass which is resolved to a B♭ forming a consonant 3rd with the bass. On the third minim beat the semibreve A forms a dissonant

A2 = 2nd alto, T1 = 1st tenor, T2 = 2nd tenor, B = bass

2nd with the bass which resolves to a consonant 3rd when the bass moves down a step to an F. These two parts form the same type of bass suspension at the start of bar 26. Another 4-3 suspension is heard between the first alto and the bass on the third beat of this bar. On the first beat of bar 27 a dissonant 7th is formed between the tied F and the dotted minim G: this resolves to a consonant 6th when the uppermost part moves to the minim E♭. Another 7-6 suspension is formed between tenor 1 and bass on the last two beats of bar 27. At the start of bar 28 the inner parts form a 2nd which resolves to a third when the tied G descends to F♯. The only case when a 4th from the bass is treated as though it were consonant is when it is approached by step, sounded on a weak beat, held through to the next strong beat then resolved downwards by step. In Example 4 the asterisk shows this consonant 4th. The two lowest parts and the lower set of figuring show that the consonant 4th is part of an unprepared 4-3 suspension. As this formula nearly always occurs at a cadence point the whole perfect cadence is sometimes called a consonant fourth cadence. This cadential progression became a cliché of late renaissance music and further examples of it may be found in bars 6, 8-9, 15, 19, 39, 46, 50, 54-55, and 67. These are all perfect cadences in G minor or the relative major, B♭, the only two keys which are confirmed by cadences. Indeed perfect cadences predominate, either as unornamented chords V and I (eg bar 3, beats 2 and 3), or with a properly prepared 4-3 suspension (eg bars 10-11). Imperfect cadences are more infrequent, but several are heard at the end of every phrase in bars 58-62. A particularly characteristic type of imperfect cadence is the Phrygian cadence (IVb-V in the minor) heard in bar 35.

The basic harmonies are decorated with off-beat passing-notes (eg the second quaver of each group of two quavers in bars 13-14) and anticipations (eg the first crotchet B♭ in bar 21 which anticipates the resolution of the suspended dotted minim C to the B♭ on the last beat of the bar). Sometimes the anticipation is itself ornamented with a lower auxiliary note. This is the case in the Phrygian cadence of bar 35. The tied D resolves on the minim C, but this resolution is anticipated by the quaver C and decorated with the lower auxiliary note B♭ between the two middle Cs. This is the case in the two final perfect cadences in bars 71-72 and 74-75 (the first quaver being an anticipation of the resolution and the second quaver being an auxiliary between the two F♯s).

Texture: Textural contrast is guaranteed by the alternation of the two choirs, one of three-part female voices, the other of four-part male voices (alto 2 being a countertenor). But within these choirs there is a great variety of texture ranging from absolute homophony (eg bar 3) to complex imitative polyphony. The latter texture is well-illustrated in Example 4. The phrase *Give me in my tormenting* in the second tenor part is imitated by the bass which maintains the same overall shape but augments the intervals between the second and third and third and fourth notes. The second alto and first tenor imitations further alter the subject, but the rhythm and pitch of the first three notes remains unchanged. This sort of freely imitative texture was the norm in vocal polyphony of the late Renaissance. The second phrase, *One kisse for my contenting* is set to a new musical phrase which starts in the bass on the second beat of bar 25 and is imitated by tenor 2, alto 2 and tenor 1 in turn with the same sort of modifications as occurred in the imitations of the first phrase. Note that the two phrases are contrapuntally overlapped in bars 25-26: alto 2 completes its first phrase by the end of bar 25, tenor 1 completes its first phrase by the second beat of bar 26, but the bass and tenor enter with the second phrase (on beats 2 and 4 of bar 25 respectively) whilst the two upper voices are still singing the first phrase. This contrapuntal overlapping was standard technique in the elaborate sacred polyphony of the period (eg LAM 3), but here it is used ironically to suggest the serious nature of Amintas' complaint (love!). The number of parts ranges from two (bars 36-37) to seven (bars 70-75). Antiphonal exchanges are most obvious in the heated exchange of bars 56-63.

Style and genre: late renaissance English madrigal.

LAM 9

Gesualdo: O vos omnes (1611)

Title and text: The title of LAM 9 is simply the first three words of a prophetic text from the Old Testament sung as darkness falls on Holy Saturday, the last night of darkness before the light and joy of Easter. In this motet Gesualdo divides the text into four phrases defined by different musical settings and techniques:

Phrase 1 *O vos omnes qui transitis per viam*: (bars 1-8)
O all you who walk this road,
Phrase 2 *Attendite, et videte*: (bars 8-14)
Take heed and look:
Phrase 3 *Si est dolor similis*: (bars 15-23)
Was ever grief
Phrase 4 *Sicut dolor meus*: (bars 23-31)
Such grief as mine?

Rhythm: In the first two phrases the rhythms are determined by word painting and a regard for the declamation of Latin. Thus the first two words are set dramatically to very long notes as though Christ were calling to us from the massive crucifix in the centre of the darkened church. There is a rhythmic ictus (like an acute accent) above the stressed syllables, and they all fall on strong beats. In phrases 3 and 4 the rhythms become more complex with faster notes decorating melodic lines which are often syncopated, eg *dolor similis* in the soprano part of bars 21-23.

Melody: The anguish of the text is reflected in the extreme angularity of the melodic lines (eg bars 4-7, first tenor) and by extreme chromaticism (eg the setting of phrase 4 in the alto part of bars 24 to the end).

Harmony: In the first phrase all of the chords are in root position with the bass falling in thirds. The chords are unrelated to each other apart from having one note in common (eg B♮ in the chords of B major and G major, bars 2 and 3). False relations are used for their dissonant effect, not as a by-product of conventional voice leading (as in LAM 4). Thus in the first three chords the soprano D♮ is immediately contradicted by the tenor D♯ which is in turn contradicted in bar 3. Note that the D♯ in bar 2 forms false relations with the soprano and first bass in bar 3 but does not form a false relation with the D♮ in the first tenor part (this is just a chromatic melodic line).

In the second phrase we hear the first real dissonance, a suspension between soprano and alto on the first beat of bar 11 (repeated with voice exchange on the first beat of bar 13).

Suspensions abound in the third phrase, some quite conventional like the 7-6 suspensions between alto and bass in bars 17 and 20, but others are less conventional. At the start of bar 18 the second tenor suspends a B♮ under an augmented triad, and when it resolves it becomes part of a second inversion triad which never resolves.

In the last phrase unrelated triads return beginning with the totally unrelated chords of B♭ major and E minor in bar 23. In bars 24-25 a pedal E in the second tenor (the real bass at this point) supports E major and A minor chords, but instead of a cadence in A minor the alto moves back to a G♯ to form the 3rd of an E minor chord and the root of the following second inversion G minor chord which resolves to a root position D major chord. The last four bars are very nearly a harmonic sequence of bars 24-27, ie a pedal B above which major and minor harmonies alternate followed by a second inversion chord of D minor resolving the A major root position chord. Although there are fleeting glimpses of keys (eg C major in bars 11-14) they are illusory. Nor can a stable mode be discerned: there are just too many chromatic inflexions to leave any semblance of modality.

Texture: The massive five and six-voice homophony in the first two phrases render the text with great clarity, while the dramatic use of silence isolates the premonitory chords of the first two bars from the rest of the setting. An imitative effect is heard at the start of the third phrase and again between first bass and soprano in bars 19-20. But there is no attempt to retain the same intervals in each successive entry (the initial semitone of *Si est* becomes a 3rd in the bass, this is inverted in the soprano, and the imitation in bars 19-20 is likewise by inversion). The last two phrases are overlapped and the texture remains densely contrapuntal until the near-homophony of the final sequences.

Style and genre: Late renaissance Latin motet.

LAM 17

Corelli: Concerto Grosso Op.6, No.8: 1st Allegro (1680)

Title: *Concerto grosso* originally meant a large group of instruments as opposed to *concertino* which was a small group of instruments. Later the term was used for the type of composition in which a *concertino* and a *concerto grosso* were featured. Here the *concertino* consists of two solo violins and a cello (the first three staves), while the *concerto grosso* (or *ripieno*) consists of two groups of violins, a group of violas and a group of cellos doubled by basses sounding an octave lower than written pitch (it is quite authentic to use single strings for the *ripieno*, but Corelli's own Roman orchestra used multiple strings). Both groups had a keyboard instrument (or other harmony instrument such as a guitar or harp) upon which improvised harmonic filling could be provided in accordance with the figured basses (one of which is realised by a modern editor on the two staves labelled cemb. = cembalo or harpsichord). The title distinguishes this genre from the baroque solo concerto (eg LAM 27). This concerto grosso was written for Christmas Eve and was intended for performance in church, one or more of its eight movements being played before, during and after Mass (the last movement is a Pastorale which is obviously meant to evoke the scene of the shepherds "watching over their flocks by night"). There were two types of concerto grosso: the *concerto da camera* (chamber concerto) had a number of dance movements, but the *concerto da chiesa* (church concerto) excluded these and was more serious in style. This is obviously a *concerto da chiesa*, so it is likely that at least one of the harmony instruments would have been an organ.

Rhythm: The music is dominated by baroque motor rhythms, with syncopated violins above a running quaver bass.

Melody: The two solo violins share the same melodic material which derives from a number of short motives. This is well-illustrated in the first four bars. The second two-bar phrase is a sequence of the first two-bar phrase with voice exchange between the two violins. The leaping 7ths in the first violin part of bars 32-39 are idiomatic to the instrument which had reached the peak of its development in the late 17th century.

Harmony: This is entirely tonal, diatonic and functional with frequent cadences. Suspensions abound and can be found by examining the figuring (in order of appearance: 6/5 = a first inversion 7th chord, 9 = a suspended 9th, 4 = a 4th from the bass, 7 = a root position 7th chord). All of them are prepared and resolved (eg in the first bar the second violin prepares the note G by sounding it as a consonance on the second beat, suspending it as a dissonance against the A in the first violin part and finally resolving it to the consonant F#). Particularly characteristic are the leap-frog suspensions of bars 9-11 and 13-15 (where the two violins jump over each other to produce the next dissonance), and the interlocking suspensions of bars 15-18. Harmonic sequences are frequent, eg bar 17 is a sequence of the previous bar, and bars 24-25 are a sequence of bars 22-23.

Tonality and form: The binary-form structure is largely determined by the key-scheme. The first half alternates between the tonic key of G minor and its relative major (B♭ major). These alternations are sometimes the result of sequences. Thus the first two bars are repeated a 3rd higher so that the key changes from G minor to B♭ major. The first section ends first with a perfect cadence (bar 19), then with a repeated Phrygian cadence (bars 20 and 21), all of them in the tonic key of G minor. In the second section the tonal scheme is more wide-ranging as Corelli explores all but one of the five most nearly-related keys: F major in bars 24-26, D minor in bars 27-29, C minor in bars 29-30 and B♭ major in bars 31-32. The movement ends with a reworking of the end of the first section, but this time the perfect cadence in the tonic is followed, not by a Phrygian cadence, but by another perfect cadence in the tonic.

Texture: The whole movement is based on the polarised texture of the concertino group which plays continuously throughout the whole movement. Indeed the work would be less interesting but would make perfectly good sense without the ripieno whose function is to reinforce the concertino, producing the terraced contrasts so characteristic of this genre. For example the second bar is an almost exact replica of the first, but contrasts with it because of the addition of the ripieno in the repeated bar: the same is true in bars 3 and 4. The ripieno group has no separate identity, the violins and bass instruments simply double their counterparts in the concertino group, while the viola supplies a subordinate harmonic filling, thus further enriching the sonority of the full band.

Style and genre: Mid-baroque concerto grosso.

LAM 21

Purcell: Dido and Aeneas: Air from Act I (1689)

Title: The first act of Purcell's opera begins with Dido's lady in waiting, Belinda, urging her mistress to shake off her melancholy. But Dido, instead of doing the sensible thing and confessing her love for Aeneas, gives her grief-stricken reply in this Air (a term for an operatic aria derived from the same French word: see LAM 16).

Rhythm: The detached notes and dotted rhythms (some of them reversed in the Lombardic style) all derive from French 17th century models (such as LAM 16), but here they are used with great effect to suggest Dido's sobbing (which cuts short the detached notes) and her mental torment (the writhing dotted rhythms almost physically representing the irregular diaphragmatic spasms of one suffering agonies of frustrated desire).

Melody: This cannot be considered in isolation from the ground bass (a bass ostinato which in this case is four bars long and is repeated six times in this extract). The melody is so constructed that it is frequently out of phase with the ground. Thus Dido's first phrase is, like the ground, four bars long and begins, like the ground, on the tonic. But Purcell starts the melody on a weak beat above the second bar of the ground and ends it in bar 5 so that it overlaps the beginning of the next statement of the ground. (This phrase contains a typically Purcellian weeping appoggiatura and an equally typical diminished 4th between the B♮ and the E♭.) Dido's next phrase is three bars long and its last bar coincides with the end of the second statement of the ground. Her third phrase (beginning in bar 9) is also four bars long so that the cadences of the ground and the vocal part again coincide. But this phrase, though similar to the first phrase, is much more passionate and reaches its climax on the high F♯ which forms a dissonant compound 7th with the bass. Although Dido's fourth phrase starts with the beginning of the ground, it is five bars long so that it again overlaps the end of one statement of the ground and the beginning of the next in bar 17. Here the dissonances formed between melody and bass come thick and fast: a 9th and a tritone on the first two beats of bar 13, an accented passing note on the first beat of bar 14 (remember that a 4th from the bass was regarded as being dissonant in the 17th century), an unresolved major 7th on the last beat of bar 14, and a 9th between the G♮ and the bass F♮ on the first beat of bar 15 (which not only does not resolve, it moves directly to another dissonance - the 7th on the second beat of bar 15). Dido's next entry (bar 20) begins above the last bar of the ground so that, although it is again four bars long, it is also out of phase with the ground, causing overlapping at bars 20-21 and 24-25. Her last phrase is five bars long so that the ground and vocal melody coincide in the last bar. Thus although the ground is absolutely four-square the music sounds almost unbroken because of the irregular phrase lengths of Dido's melody and the way the two only coincide three times. A bonus of this skilful out-of-phase phrasing is that Purcell is able to introduce some subtle imitation between treble and bass (the ground imitating the vocal part in bars 21-22 and 25-26) thus further cementing the unity of the two parts.

Harmony and tonality: Purcell wrote just the treble and bass of this Air (without figuring), leaving it to the harpsichordist to improvise harmonic filling. However the ground itself suggests functional harmony such as I Vb I/V VI Ib/IV V (with a conventional 4-3 suspension which is forced on the harpsichordist/editor by Dido's appoggiatura) and I. But Purcell's harmonic style is much more eccentric and interesting than this (as the dissonances between treble and bass suggest). The modern editor has responded brilliantly to the clues Purcell gives. Thus after the straightforward harmonisation I have suggested (and which the modern editor uses), he treats the first note of the ground as a bass suspension in bar 5, harmonises it with chord VIb in bar 9 (thus disguising the end of one statement of the ground and the start of the next). Amongst many other felicities he takes the hint from Purcell and introduces his own snatch of imitation in bars 17-18 (where the uppermost part of the harpsichord realisation imitates the ground after two beats). Although the music never leaves the tonic key of C minor the skill of Purcell and his modern editor means that there is no lack of variety in this magnificent music.

Texture: Polarised two-part counterpoint between tune and bass with harmonic filling provided by the harpsichordist.

Style and genre: A continuo air in English restoration style.

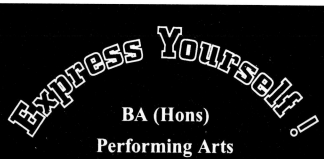

LAM 23

Couperin: Les Sentiments, Sarabande (1713)

Title and performance direction: *Les sentiments* = feelings, *très tendrement* = very tenderly. By the late 17th/early 18th centuries the sarabande had become a stylised, slow, serious and stately dance in triple time. Couperin wrote that "the titles [of his harpsichord pieces] correspond with the ideas I had [and] one should note that the pieces which carry titles are like portraits ...". Thus we have a fairly clear idea about how the music should be interpreted: it should convey tender emotions seriously through the medium of a slow tempo and delicately performed ornamentation. Although predominantly in the major, the phrase in A minor (bars 13-16) should give an insight into the depth of emotion which is disguised by these sophisticated *agréments*.

Melody: Entirely diatonic and falling into four balanced eight-bar phrases, each of them consisting of a four-bar antecedent and a four-bar consequent. A simple melody (shown in Example 23) is encrusted with ornamentation (the interpretation of which is shown in the *Appendix* to the *Anthology*). It is unified by repetitions of subtly varied motives which are also shown in Example 23 (yI in bar 22 is a melodic inversion of y).

Historical context: François Couperin le grand (the adjective added to distinguish him from an earlier relative with the same name) was the last and greatest of a family of composers whose ancestry can be traced back to the early 17th century. His huge corpus of harpsichord music represents the pinnacle of achievement of the classical French harpsichord school (confusingly the French refer to the reign of Louis XIV - for whom Couperin worked at Versailles - as the classical era). He was as famous as Corelli throughout Europe and his style was imitated by Bach in such music as the Air and French Overture from the *Goldberg Variations* (LAM 35a).

Ex. 23

Harmony, tonality and form: Apart from one chord (Vb of V in bar 11 which could be analysed as passing notes between Ib and V) the harmony is entirely diatonic. Of the 40 chords shown in the harmonic analysis (Example 23), 17 are tonic chords and 17 are dominants (including VIIb which is, in effect, an incomplete dominant 7th). The other chords (VI, IV, III/II, VIb and II⁷b in order of appearance) are all of subdominant function and all proceed, as expected, to tonic or dominant chords. This diatonic, functional harmony creates a clearly-defined tonal structure, and the tonal structure together with the melody creates a binary form of utmost clarity:

A: bars 1-8
  Antecedent ending with a perfect cadence in the tonic +
  Consequent ending with a perfect cadence in the dominant
B1: bars 9-16
  Antecedent ending with an imperfect cadence in the tonic +
  Consequent ending with a perfect cadence in the supertonic
B2: bars 17-24
  Antecedent ending with an imperfect cadence in the tonic +
  Consequent ending with a perfect cadence in the tonic

To this is added, as was the French custom, a *petite reprise*, ie a repetition of B2 in bars 25-32.

It will be seen that the harmonic rhythm emphasises the triple metre of the dance. There is a change of chord at every barline except after the cadences in bars 4 and 8. A change of chord tends to engender an accent on the second of the two chords, ie on the first beat of the bar. Within each bar the most frequent harmonic rhythm is minim-crotchet which again emphasises triple time (a long note on the strong beat followed by a short note on the weak beat). The other harmonic rhythms within the bar are dotted minims (which clearly emphasise the first beat of the bar). Only once (bar 3) does the harmony change every beat, and this does not disturb the already-established triple-time harmonic rhythm. Some text books will tell you that a characteristic of the sarabande was an accent on the second beat of the bar. This is by no means a general rule, and only twice (bars 13 and 15) is such an accent suggested by a harmonic rhythm of crotchet-minim (ie a short note on the first beat and a long note on the second beat, thus throwing more weight on the second beat of the bar).

Ornamentation: Couperin's conventional symbols are fully explained in the *Appendix*, but it remains to consider the melodic ornaments which are fully written-out and which form a part of the simple melody underlying the florid *agréments*. These are shown above the first stave of Example 23. In order of appearance they are:

e = échappée or escape note (bar 1). This is a metrically-weak and dissonant ornament which moves away from the harmony note (or essential note) by step, then returns to another harmony note by leaping a 3rd. Here the first harmony note (B♮) is the 3rd of chord I. The échappée is a step above this and forms a dissonant 7th with the D in chord I. The melodic line then leaps a 3rd to reach the consonant A♮ in chord Vb.

p = passing note. This is a metrically weak ornament between two harmony notes a 3rd apart. The passing note comes between the G♮ of chord VI and the B♮ of chord Ib. It is dissonant with the B♮ in chord VI.

a = anticipation. This is a metrically-weak dissonant note which immediately precedes a note of the same pitch, usually at a barline in a cadence. The semiquaver A is dissonant with chord I and it anticipates the consonant minim A after the barline. The quaver D at the end of the phrase is dissonant with chord V and it anticipates the consonant dotted-minim D after the barline.

s = suspension. This is a dissonance on a strong beat which is prepared by being tied over from the same note sounding as a consonance. It is resolved by moving to another harmony note, usually by step. This is the case in bars 6^3-7^2 where the suspension is prepared (P) as a consonant note in the accompanying D major chord, suspended (S) as a dissonance above the A major chord, then resolved (R) by step down to the consonant C♯ (the 3rd of the accompanying A major chord). Sometimes suspensions are decorated by leaping to another consonant harmony note before turning back to the normal note of resolution. This is the case in bar 5^3-6^3 where the suspended E♮ ducks down to the consonant harmony note (A♮) before reaching its eventual goal, the resolution to the tied D♮ (which is both a resolution of the first suspension and a preparation for the second).

Texture and style: The density of the texture varies from two to five voices (or even six and seven voices if the sustained notes are counted). The predominantly homophonic texture is enlivened by some melodic movement in the lower part which briefly suggests counterpoint. This movement in the lower parts, together with the florid ornamentation, is partly an attempt to overcome the fact that harpsichords are incapable of sustained sounds of any significant length. This sort of texture is known as *style brisé* (broken style) which was first developed on fretted instruments such as the lute: by the end of the 17th century it had become one of the most obvious characteristics of the music of *les clavecinistes français* (the French harpsichord school).

LAM 34

Handel: Messiah, No. 41 Chorus (1742)

Title: The Messiah was (and to Christians, still is) the redeemer who was born and suffered as a man in order to reconcile us to God. The oratorio falls in to three parts, not unlike the three acts of the Italian operas with which Handel made his fame in early 18th century London. It tells the story of the world's redemption mainly through prophetic Old Testament texts. These Handel set using the genres developed in contemporary opera: recitative and aria. The work differs from the baroque opera in the emphasis placed on the chorus. Indeed the choral music nearly always forms the dramatic climax of scenes which begin with the usual recitative-aria pair. Towards the end of Part 2, scene 5 tells how the Gospel (the good news of Christ's life, death and resurrection) was spread by the apostles in the famous aria *How beautiful are the feet of them that preach the Gospel of peace* and the chorus *Their sound is gone out into all lands*. But the good news was not always well-received, and scene 6 consists of a pair of movements which are among them most dramatic Handel ever wrote. The first is a bass aria which expresses astonishment at the hostile reception which the apostles encountered (*Why do the nations so furiously rage together ... against the Lord and against his Anointed?*). The second is our chorus *Let us break their bonds asunder, and cast away their yokes from us*. The bonds which are to be broken by the Apostles are the bonds of sin, and the yokes which the Apostles will cast off are the false philosophies and beliefs of the pagan world. Like most baroque movements LAM 34 expresses one affection, that of righteous rage at the false gods of the pagans.

Ex. 34a   Let us break their bonds asunder

Rhythm: The trochaic metre (strong-weak, strong-weak etc.) of *Let us break their bonds asunder* is wonderfully conveyed by motive x (Example 34a) in which the effort of singing the higher of the two notes (especially at the start) is bound to create a rhythmic effect which almost physically suggests someone hacking at prisoners' shackles. In Example 34a the dashes and horse-shoes above the text represent strong and weak accents respectively, and the bar-lines divide the text into four trochaic feet. But English declamation is more complex than this. A good actor would never give equal weight to all of these stressed syllables (though strong-weak accentuation would be maintained in the background). The actor would choose one or two syllables which would receive a mega-accent, and differing accentuations could alter the sense of the sentence. Thus if the actor chose *bonds* for the only mega-accent it would give the sentence a sense that *bonds* had been carefully selected from a range of alternatives, such as cages or leg-irons. But if the actor chose *break* for the only mega-accent it could suggest that the listener was being urged to break the bonds rather than, for instance, to cut or burn them. Now it is clear that, because the soprano and tenor are out of phase in the first three bars, the alignment of the barlines in triple time is only a matter of convenience. Let us suppose our actor decides that the mega-accents should come on *break* and the second syllable of *asunder*, then over and above the trochaic feet the rhythm indicated by the stress marks and barlines under the text in Example 34a would have been adopted. If we apply this to Handel's music then a much more complex and exciting combination of rhythm emerges. This is indicated by the printed music in Example 34a. The sopranos effectively perform their part in 2/4 time (because a barline should come before each of the mega-stresses indicated by the dashes). To accommodate the extra beat in the tenor part, a bar of 3/4 time is needed. What results from the combination of the two parts is a series of mega-stresses alternating between the tenor and soprano, the two parts only coming together on the word *break* at the start of bar 3 of LAM 34 (thereby suggesting that Handel himself thought this word should take a mega-accent). It is this "polymetre" which drives the music forward so relentlessly and powers the stretti of the cataclysmic climaxes.

The rhythms of the second subject (Example 34b) contrast strongly with those in the first subject. More importantly these rhythms now clearly define triple time. This is essential, for only against a clearly established triple metre can Handel's last rhythmic effect, the hemiolas in bars 52-53, 57-58 and 65-67, be clearly distinguished.

Ex. 34b

Melody: There are two subjects, one for each phrase of the text. The first subject is shown in Example 34a. It is built out of two motives, the first (x) a falling 4th extended in a descending sequence, the second (y) a semiquaver figure sometimes being treated in sequence (soprano bar 2) and sometimes being omitted altogether (bars 54-55). Other alterations are made for practical purposes, eg instead of continuing the sequence of x in the first tenor entry the falling 4th is intervallically inverted to become a rising 5th (see Example 34a). This is done so that the tenors will not have to sing uncomfortably low, so that the space between the two parts will not become too wide, and so that the bass entry (shown by a direct) will not be obscured by the tenors singing below it.

The second subject starts at bar 10 and, as Example 34b shows, it is made out of three motives. Motive x is a dramatic figure of falling 3rds which encompasses the interval of a 7th: this is never repeated or treated in sequence in any version of the second subject. Motive y is treated in sequence, but in bars 35-40 Handel modifies the subject by extending just the semiquavers in a much longer sequence. Motive z is also treated in sequence and is used as a countermelody against motives x and y. This subject, like the first, is very angular and rhythmically powerful so that it again conveys the physicality of the text.

Harmony and tonality: The harmony is (with one exception) entirely diatonic and almost entirely consonant. Its functional simplicity clarifies the tonal structure, and the tonal structure (using only closely related major keys) in turn clarifies the form of the whole movement.

Texture, tonality and form: The whole movement consists of a tightly woven web of imitative counterpoint. Only at the hemiolas do the parts come together for homophonic cadences. The most important means of generating increasing energy is the use of stretto. The alternation of the two subjects determines the form, but this, as has already been mentioned, is clarified by the tonal scheme.

Section A (bars 1-9): C major ➤ G major ➤ D major
The voices sing the first subject imitatively in pairs at the interval of a beat, the second pair entering after two bars and overlapping the first by one beat in bar 3. When this point of imitation begins again in G major (bar 5) the second pair enter in stretto just one bar after the first pair. The violins (which have hitherto doubled the sopranos and altos) provide a link to:

Section B (bars 10-23): G major
The whole of the second subject as shown in Example 34b is heard in strict canon at the 5th above, between the tenors and altos, and the canon is overlapped by the soprano entry. The final entry (bass, bar 18) is tonal, ie the first interval is diminished from a 3rd to a semitone.

Section A1 (bars 23-34): G major ➤ F major ➤ C major ➤ G major
Motive x of the first subject is treated in close stretto before the whole subject returns in the tonic in bars 29-31. The violins again link this section to:

Section B1 (bars 35-44): C major ➤ F major ➤ C major
The second subject is treated in stretto (at an interval of just one beat), and this overlaps with the bass entry followed by the alto entry two bars later.

The violins again link this section to the next and overlap it by a bar and a beat.

Section C (bars 45-59): G major ➤ C major The two subjects are now brought into closer proximity, the climax being reached when motive x of the second subject is treated in the closest possible stretto in the entries marked ff in bars 47-48. The hemiolaic cadences of bars 52-54 and 57-59 mark the final definitive return to the tonic key of C major.

Orchestral coda (bars 59-67): C major
Final stretti of both subjects.

Style and genre: Contrapuntal chorus from a late baroque oratorio.

LAM 35

Bach: Goldberg Variations (1742)

Title: Goldberg was a virtuoso organist and harpsichordist who was in the service of the Russian ambassador to the court of Dresden. It is said that Goldberg played selections from these Variations every night to help the insomniac ambassador get to sleep. The ambassador richly rewarded both composer and performer. The Variations take the form of a massive passacaglia built on the opening binary-form Aria, ie a work in which the form, phrase lengths, underlying harmonic progression and an outline of the bass are maintained in each variation, while the affection, compositional technique, and melodies of each variation differ radically from the Aria. Explanations of the titles above each variation will be found in the *Appendix* to the *Anthology*.

Rhythm:
Aria: The complexity of the melodic rhythms show that this movement is in French baroque style (cf LAM 23). The dotted rhythms, including the Scotch snaps in bar 7, are particularly characteristic. The style is that of a sarabande and this is more apparent in this movement than it is in Couperin's *Sarabande* (LAM 23) since a subtle second-beat accent is engendered by the rhythmic articulation of the melody in bars 1, 3, 5, 9 and 11 (in all of these bars a single detached crotchet on the first beat is followed by legato phrasing or a longer note on the second beat of the bar). This melodic complexity contrasts with the simple bass line – simple so that it will be remembered in the variations.
Variations 10 and 21: The simplicity of the rhythms in these two movements is necessary, otherwise the complex counterpoint would be swamped.
Variation 29: Bach ensures that the descending bass at the start of the ground is clear by beginning bars 1, 2, 3, 5 and 6 with quavers in a low register which contrast with the virtuosic semiquaver chords in a high register. The triplet signs in bar 4 apply to the rest of the bar, and those in bar 8 apply to bars 9-15 as well (it is a convention that once triplets have been established there is no need to keep repeating the figure 3). In bars 4 and 8 the dotted rhythms are conventionally equalised with the triplets in the right hand, ie the demisemiquavers are made to coincide with the last note of each triplet group (this principle of equalisation does not always apply in baroque music, but here sheer speed dictates that the convention should apply).

Melody:
Aria: The already florid melody is further decorated with ornaments designated by conventional symbols, possible interpretations of which are given in the *Appendix* to the *Anthology*. Example 35a shows the two motives which recur as follows:

> bars 3-4: repeat of x an octave lower and further decoratedbars
> 5-6: repeat of x transposed down a 4th
> bars 9-10: repeat of x transposed down a 6th and with y modified by the equalisation of the falling figure and the omission of the appoggiatura variants of y at the start of bars 13, 14 and 15.

Variation 10: The start of the fugal subject not only contains the first two notes of the ground (circled in Example 35b), it is a skeletal version of the melody of the first two bars of the Aria (as a comparison of Examples 35a and 35b reveals). The rest of the subject is constructed around the next two notes of the ground. **Variation 21:** The chromaticism of this minor mode variation is apparent in all three parts.
Variation 29: Melody is strikingly absent and is replaced by toccata-like chords and triplet figuration.

Harmony, tonality and form:

Aria: Example 35c shows the bass of the Aria and shows how the most important notes from it are used in Variations 10 (Example 35e), 21 (Example 35f) and 29 (Example 35g). These examples show that beneath the decorations in the bass of the Aria and all variations there is a simple one-note-per-bar bass (shown in Example 35d) the notes of which are common to all sections of the passacaglia (though this bass is never heard in its raw form). The Roman numerals under the stave in Example 35d show Bach's harmonic progression in the Aria. In bars 3-4 there is an imperfect cadence in the tonic key of G major and in bars 7-8 a perfect cadence in G. Together these two phrases constitute a perfectly balanced antecedent and consequent. The third phrase (bars 9-12) begins in G but modulates via the pivot chord in bar 10 to reach an imperfect cadence in the dominant key of D major in bars 11-12. As in the first two phrases this antecedent is balanced by a consequent which concludes with a perfect cadence (bars 15-16) now in the dominant. It is these cadences which most clearly define the periodic phrase structure of this, the first part of a binary-form movement (the second half modulates back to the tonic, but is not shown in the *Anthology*).

Variations: As with the bass, so with the harmonic progressions which are maintained with some modifications in all of the variations. The modifications do not alter the phrase structure, they consist of new chords which are functionally equivalent to the corresponding chords in the Aria. Apart from different inversions of the same chord the only change in the harmony of Variation 10 is the use of chord IV in the first two beats of bar 14 (instead of chord IIb in bar 14 of Example 35d). Every bar of Variation 21 is equivalent to two bars in the Aria, and because it is in the tonic minor the harmony differs to a greater extent. These changes involve adding extra chords between most of those in the Aria as well as changing the original chords (though their function remains the same). Thus the implicit or explicit harmonic progression of the first phrase is I, VIb, V^{m9}, vb/ivb^7, IVb, V^7 (little Roman numerals indicate chords derived from the melodic minor). Here chord VIb has been inserted between chords I and Vb, and Vb itself has been replaced by an incomplete dominant minor 9th (V^{m9}). Again a chord has been added on the last beat of the first bar, and ivb^7 and IVb replace chord VIIb of V, but the imperfect cadence remains intact. More radically three notes of the ground are omitted in the remainder of this variation. At the start of bar 3 a B♭ in the bass would have sounded ugly against the same note in the alto (which is needed for the canon), so Bach drops to the root instead of the third of the chord. The same is true of the third beat of bar 5 (root D instead of 3rd F). In the minor the supertonic (E♭) would form a tritone with the dominant (A), so Bach completely abandons the passacaglia bass and harmony for just one note (compare the bass notes E and A in bars 11-12 of the Aria with the B♭ and A on beats 1 and 2 of bar 6 of this variation).

In bars 3-4 of Variation 21 Bach gives a lesson in functional harmony. The essential harmony at the end of phrase 1 in the Aria and all of the variations is an imperfect cadence in G. This can be achieved by using chords VIIb of V and V itself (as in bars 3-4 of the Aria), or II^7 and V (as is implied in bars 3-4 of Variation 10), or IVb and V (as in bars 1-2 of Variation 21). A further possibility is VI and V. Bach uses chord VI at the start of bar 3 in Variation 29, but he finishes the bar with the chord used in bar 3 of the Aria (VIIb of V) thus demonstrating the subdominant function of both of these chords.

Textures:

Aria: Style brisé.

Fughetta = a little fugue. The extract consists of a four-voice fugal exposition in which the answers (tenor, bars 5-8 and alto, bars 13-16) are tonal, ie the interval labelled "tone" in Example 35b becomes a 3rd in the corresponding bars of the answers. Because of the harmonic progressions, Bach is unable to bring the final entry in at the "correct" pitch for an answer (starting on a D♯ like the first four bars of the tenor part). The texture, as in all fugal expositions, is consistently contrapuntal.

Canone alla Settima = canon at the 7th. The dux starts in the tenor in bar 1, the comes in the same bar in the treble. Example 35f reveals that the bass includes nearly all of the notes of the ground, but Bach skilfully incorporates the opening figure of the canonic parts and other figuration derived from them so that the texture for the most part is three-voice counterpoint.

Variatio 29 a 1 ovvero 2 Clav. = Variation 29 for one or two keyboards. It is possible (just!) to play this variation on a one-manual harpsichord (or even on a piano as Glen Gould so brilliantly demonstrated), but the texture of alternating three-part chords is obviously inspired by the potential of a two-manual

harpsichord. This toccata contrasts three types of texture, alternating chords, two-part counterpoint (bars 4, 8 and 15) and monophonic figuration.

Styles and genres: French sarabande with variations taking the forms of a fughetta, a canon and a toccata.

LAM 36

CPE Bach: Württemberg Sonata No.5: 3rd Movement (1743)

Title: This is the fifth of six keyboard sonatas dedicated to the Duke of Württemberg, a German princeling whose seat was Stuttgart.

Rhythm and melody: Almost entirely diatonic and based upon a few motives which are casually manipulated here and there. Example 36a shows how motive a of bars 1 and 2 is altered by augmenting its intervals in bars 10-12, and how the little three-note rhythm x reappears at the end of the extract. Motive b (Example 36b) is immediately repeated in bars 4-6 then resurfaces in C minor in bars 24-26 (still outlining a dominant 7th chord resolving on the third degree of the scale). This version is immediately repeated in the sequence of bars 26-28. Motive c (Example 36c) is heard in a modified sequence (bars 7-8) and is then inverted (bars 8-9). The rest is hardly melodic, it consists simply of pretty figurations outlining the harmonic progressions and cliché appoggiaturas of this style (eg the first beats of bars 14, 16 and 17.

Harmony: Mostly diatonic with a slow rate of change which speeds up towards the cadences. For example, the harmonic progression of the first ten bars is: I / V^b/ V^7 / Ib / V^7 / Ib / Vb / I / Ib VIIb I / Ic V (obliques = barlines). For the first eight bars the harmony changes at most once per bar, but in bar 9 there are three chords and in bar 10 there are two. The analysis reveals the extent to which Bach relies upon tonic and dominant chords. It also shows the cadential 6/4 which is heard again in both of the feminine cadences in bars 10 and 18, and the masculine cadence at the end of the extract.

Tonality and form: Simple functional harmonies define the tonal structure:
   Bars 1-10: E♭ major ending with an imperfect cadence,
   Bars 10-18: E♭ major modulating to an imperfect cadence in the dominant key of B♭ major,
   Bars 18-42: B♭ major with transitory modulations to C minor (bars 25-26) and D minor (bars 27-28 are a sequence of bars 25-26), then through a circle of fifths (bars 28-30) to G minor (bars 30-31) before the dominant pedal of B♭ major (bars 32-40) and the final perfect cadence in the dominant key of B♭ major.

   None of the transitory modulations in bars 18-42 disturb the feeling that the whole section is in B♭ major, indeed they could all be regarded as secondary dominants resolving onto diatonic chords in B♭ major, eg the harmony of bars 25-26 could be regarded as being V^7 of II resolving to chord II. This is the first section of a movement in two parts, the second of which develops the motives of LAM 36 before recapitulating motive a and the last 18 bars of page 119 transposed down a 5th so that the movement ends in the tonic. Even without knowing the structure of the second part, the tonal scheme of our extract suggests that it might well be the exposition of a sonata form movement in which bars 1-10 form the first subject in the tonic, bars 10-18 form a transition which modulates to the dominant, and bars 18-42 form the second subject in the dominant. There is not, however, clearly differentiated thematic material, in fact the opening of the second subject (bars 18-24) is a repeat of bars 2-8 transposed up a 5th. What we have here then is the first part of a movement which is transitional between Bachian binary form (eg LAM 35) and classical sonata form (eg LAM 42).

Texture: Largely in two parts, one of them being subservient to the other (eg motive b which is heard against a pedal). At structural points (the start, the end of the first subject/beginning of the transition, and the end of the exposition) the texture thickens as four, five and six-part chords are introduced.

Style and genre: Galant keyboard sonata.

LAM 42

Clementi: Keyboard Sonata in G minor, Op.7, No.3 (1782)

Title: Although Clementi's Op.7 is entitled *Three Sonatas for pianoforte or harpsichord*, the extreme dynamic marks (including *forzando* accents) show that it was conceived for the piano (Clementi was an astute business man, and he would not have wished to preclude customers who only possessed a harpsichord from buying his sonatas).

Rhythm, motive and melody: Clementi's melodies are often constructed by manipulating one or two tiny motives. Example 42a (ii) shows how variants of the three-note rhythmic motive x overlap to form the first four bars of an eight-bar phrase. These are interrupted by a three-note hammering figure (z), before x returns, followed by a cadential figure ending on the leading-note. This is an

Ex. 42a   Augmentation of first subject of first movement in bars 102-109

(i)

(ii) bars 1-8

(iii)

(iv)

(v)

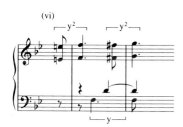

(vi)

eight-bar antecedent which is answered by an eight-bar consequent which is a repetition of the first phrase up to bar 15. At this point the expected perfect cadence is dramatically avoided by an interrupted cadence. In order to complete the musical sense Clementi repeats the melody of the cadence, but this time he harmonises it with a perfect cadence (bars 19-20).

The whole of the first movement (and even the whole sonata) is unified by a syncopated two-note motive (y in Example 42a (ii)). Its characteristic rhythm (a short off-beat accented note followed by a longer on-beat note) is illustrated in Examples 42a (the first movement), 42b (the slow movement) and 42c (the finale). Motive y[1] (Example 42a (iii) and (iv)) underpins the first melody of the second subject (bars 22-28) and appears in a very syncopated form in bars 36-40. Motive y^1 is inverted (Example 42a (v) and (vi)) in bars 44 and 53 (left hand), 58-60, 62-64, 66-69 and above the tonic pedal (bars 74-80) at the end of the exposition. Example 42d shows how Clementi combines all three motives in bars 43-45. These are but a few instances of Clementi's motivic integration and development.

In the first movement the melody of the periodically-phrased first subject (bars 1-20) is entirely diatonic, but its *Sturm und Drang* style contrasts with the galant style of the first theme of the second subject (bars 21-28). Each balanced four-bar phrase is decorated with chromatic appoggiaturas (bars 24 and 28). These elegant decorations contrast with the syncopated chromatic appoggiatura in bar 40 (a version of motive y). The only extended lyrical melody in the first movement is the theme in bars 102-117, but even this turns out to be an augmentation of the first subject in the relative major (as a comparison of (i) and (ii) in Example 42a will reveal).

Ex. 42b Cantabile e lento, bars 15-16   **Ex. 42c** Presto, bars 24-26

Ex. 42d Allegro con spirito, bars 43-45

The ornate melodies of the slow movement's opening bars appear to be spontaneously lyrical, but even here Clementi cannot resist motivic integration. Underlying the melody in bars 1 and 3 is a four-note descending scale (x in Example 42e) which is treated imitatively in bars 5-6 (Example 42e (ii)). In bar 12 a little linking figure combines motive y^2 from the first movement with a new motive (z in Example 24e (iii)). The theme of the second subject (starting at bar 13) is forged from motives x and z (as Example 42e (iv) shows).

The themes of the finale are really no more than cleverly deployed scales which persist even in the second subject (eg the bass in bars 16-19), but the connection

Ex. 42e Unifying motives in Canabile e lento

(i) bar 1

(ii) bars 5-6

(iii) bar 12   (iv) bars 13-14

42

between motive y of the first subject and the second theme of the second subject of the finale (bars 24-29) should be remembered. Rhythmically this movement contains the most complex syncopations. These are caused by a cross-phrased melody in bars 24-30 and by the almost Bartókian accents on the second and fifth quavers in bars 69 and 71.

Harmony: The clear functional harmony of the classical period is always evident. So too are classical Ic-V^7-I cadences (eg first movement, bars 49-50). But grinding dissonances and dramatic chromatic chords are more evident than in the music of any other composer writing in the 1780's. As soon as bar 6 a very exposed 9-8 suspension is highlighted by a sudden forte, and this is followed by a secondary dominant (V^{7}b of V Example 42a (ii)). The forzando in bar 40 is more dramatic than the two previous accents because motive y is harmonised with a chromatic diminished 7th chord (a minor 9th chord in B$^\flat$ major). The lead back to the dominant chord of G minor at the end of the development is achieved by an augmented 6th chord in bar 161. The final cadences of the first movement are interrupted by startlingly dramatic diminished 7th chords (V^{m9} of IV in bars 206 and 210).

In the slow movement chromaticism and dissonance are even more obvious because of the way they interrupt the serene flow of the melodies, eg the diminished 7th chord in bar 7 and the double appoggiaturas in the first beat of bar 11 (B$\natural$ and D$\natural$ against the E$^\flat$ of chord IIb in B$^\flat$ major).

Highly dissonant appoggiaturas are strongly featured in the finale: in bars 62-64 there is an appoggiatura on the first beat of every bar, and in the following two bars they appear on every dotted-crotchet beat. As in the first movement Clementi prepares for the recapitulation with an augmented 6th chord, this time in third inversion (bar 79).

A final characteristic of Clementi's harmony is his predilection for pedal points. The first and second movements begin with a tonic pedal, the beginning of the second subject of the first movement (bars 22-28) revolves around an inner pedal (F$\natural$) decorated with motive y, a dominant pedal (bars 59-68) generates expectation for the cadence in B major, and when this appears (bars 73-74) it is immediately followed by a tonic pedal (bars 74-80).

Texture: Clementi totally avoids the clichés of galant melody-plus-Alberti bass of composers such as JC Bach (eg LAM 41). Instead he uses the full range of the late 18th century pianoforte with the virtuosity for which he was justly famed. The amazing variety of textures may be judged by the following examples:
- melody plus bass, both in octaves - a particularly bare texture much favoured by Clementi (eg bars 17-18 in the slow movement),
- parallel 3rds and 6ths doubled at the octave (eg bars 39-40 in the slow movement),
- two-part counterpoint doubled at the octave (eg bars 67-75 in the finale),
- melody cross-phrased over broken chords with sustained notes to create a conjunct bass (eg bars 90-95 in the finale),
- four-part chords over virtuosic bass octaves (eg bars 1-5 in the finale),
- virtuosic scales in tenths (eg bars 71-72 in the first movement),
- octave melody over broken chords and a pedal in the left hand (eg bars 102-117 in the first movement),
- massive chordal interjections in up to 10 parts (eg bar 206 of the first movement).

Tonality and form: Clementi's exploration of remote keys was more daring than any of his contemporaries. This is evident in his use of the Neapolitan key of G$\sharp$ minor (finale, bars 50ff) in a movement in G minor (strictly speaking the Neapolitan key is the flat supertonic, but A$^\flat$ minor is such an infernally difficult key to decipher, that Clementi uses its enharmonic equivalent as a matter of convenience). This passage is part of a tumultuous development section which passes rapidly through other unrelated and related keys: elsewhere his tonal structures are more conventional.

All three movements are in sonata form, but none of them come as near as JC Bach's movement (LAM 41) to the generally accepted norm which 19th century theorists supposed a majority of classical composers used. As is often the case, tonality determines structure to a greater extent than the deployment of themes and motives (which, as we have seen, often invade more than one section of a movement).

First Movement: Sonata form in G minor
Exposition (bars 1-80): G minor and B$^\flat$ major

First subject (bars 1-20): G minor. There is no transition.

Second subject (bars 21-74): B$^\flat$ major. There are three principal thematic groups, each of them unified with each other and with the first subject by the use of motives y (see Example 42a), x and z (see Example 42d): a galant theme accompanied by motive y (bars 21-28), an eight-bar melody featuring Mozartian melodic chromaticism (bars 43-50 with a modified repeat), with references to motives x and z, a repeated four-bar theme fashioned from motive y which, at the second repeat, is extended to reach the dominant (bars 58-70). These themes are linked with each other and with the codetta by non-thematic scales and developments of motive y.

Codetta (bars 74-80): B♭ major. A version of motive x (right hand) is heard above motive y over a tonic pedal.

Development (bars 81-168): B♭ major to G minor

Bars 81-88: the first four bars of the first subject in B♭ major are answered by a new figure in octaves which modulates to C minor.

Bars 89-96: a modified repeat of the previous eight bars, starting in C minor and ending on V^{m9} of B♭.

Bars 97-117: a linking passage leads to an augmentation of the first four bars of the first subject in E♭ major (immediately repeated).

Bars 117-122: another link consists of dominant and tonic chords in A♭ major and (sequentially) in B♭ major.

Bars 123-141: dominant preparation for E♭ major.

Bars 142-167: False recapitulation of the second theme of the second subject in E♭ major followed by an extension of bars 36-42 to lead to chord V of G minor.

Recapitulation (bars 169-214): G minor. An almost exact repeat of the first subject shorn of its interrupted cadence is followed immediately by the third theme of the second subject (bars 184-200 = 58-74 transposed to the tonic key of G minor). The coda is delayed by dramatic secondary dominants and repetitions of the perfect cadence.

Coda (bars 214-220 = 74-80): G minor.

Slow movement: Abridged sonata form in E♭ major. All sections are motivically linked (see Example 42e).

Exposition (bars 1-20): E♭ major and B♭ major.

First Subject (bars 1-4): E♭ major. Transition (bars 5-12): E♭ major modulating to B♭ major.

Second Subject (bars 13-20): B♭ major.

There is no development, instead a 7th and a minor 9th are added to chord V (bar 20, beat 2) to link the second subject to the recapitulation.

Recapitulation (bars 21-46): E♭ major with transitory modulations to C minor and A♭ major in the transition. Bars 21-24 = 1-4. In the transition (bars 25-38) the abrupt move to the relative minor (bars 25-26) and the chromatic slither to the subdominant (bars 27-29) together with another chromatic slither to V of E♭ (bars 35-38) make this section sound more like a development. In the second subject bars 39-46 = 13-20 transposed to the tonic.

Coda (bars 46-48): E♭ major (cf coda of first movement).

Finale: Sonata form in G minor.

Exposition (bars 1-40): G minor and B♭ major.

First Subject (bars 1-8): G minor.

Transition (bars 9-15): G minor modulating through C minor to B♭ major.

Second Subject (bars 16-33): B♭ major.

Bars 16-24: an eight-bar phrase consisting of the scalic figure from the first subject with a new countermelody followed by scalic figuration.

Bars 24-30: a cross-phrased theme derived from motive y of the first movement (see Example 42c).

Bars 30-33: a repeat of the scalic figuration of bars 20-23.

Codetta (bars 34-40): B♭ major. Inversions of the bass of the first subject over a tonic pedal.

Development (bars 41-80): B♭ major modulating through E♭ minor, A♭ minor/G♯ minor and D minor to V of G minor. The figure from the beginning of the transition (cf bars 9 and 41) is heard over a pedal which changes function from being a tonic pedal in B♭ major to becoming the bass of V^7 in E♭ minor in bar 44. The melodic sequence initiated in these bars continues in the next four-bar phrase (which ends on V^7 of A♭ minor). In bars 50-57 the whole of the first subject is re-stated in G♯ minor (the enharmonic equivalent of A♭ minor). A sequential development of the opening figure of the transition (bars 58-66) passes through A minor and D minor. At this point (bar 67) Clementi develops the first subject in two-part counterpoint passing through G minor (bars 71-72), then sequentially through E♭ major and C minor (bars 73 and 74 respectively), before cadencing in G minor (bars 75 -76). The development ends with an imperfect cadence in this tonic key.

Recapitulation (bars 80-100): G minor. Clementi omits the first subject and repeats only bars 24-34 of the first subject (which he repeats with an intensification of the syncopated figures in bars 90-100).

Coda (bars 100-106): G minor. The inversion of the first subject used in the codetta is here re-inverted to its original form (compare the left hand part of bars 1-3 with the right hand part of bars 100-102). The opening of this scalic figure is imitated in the left hand part (bars 101-102 and 104-105).

LAM 45

Mozart: Piano Concerto in D minor, K466: 1st Movement (1785)

Title: By Mozart's time the piano had become the instrument of choice for keyboard concertos: it is impossible to imagine that this work could have been adequately performed on a harpsichord. K466 is the number by which this concerto is identified in Köchel's catalogue of Mozart's works.

Rhythm: The syncopation in the upper strings (bars 91-105) links this concerto with Haydn's *Lamentatione Symphony* (LAM 40), but the rhythm is even more agitated than Haydn's because it continues for 15 instead of 8 bars and there is no on-beat crotchet bass such as that which supports the opening bars of the symphony. The scalic interjections of the lower strings only add to the tension which the pianist's Beethovenian motor rhythms do nothing to dispel.

Melody: The diatonic piano melody of bars 77-86 falls into two-bar phrases, but the phrases of the accompanying chords are out of phase with the melody so that they overlap the periodic phrasing to produce a seamless flow. The yearning melancholy of the melody can be attributed, at least in part, to the wide leaps (of up to a 10th), the implied appoggiaturas at the start of every even-numbered bar, and the use of augmented 2nds (derived from the harmonic minor scale) in bars 82 and 87.

This lyrical melody contrasts with the theme of the first subject (bars 91-108). It bears a striking resemblance to the opening of Haydn's *Lamentatione Symphony*, being similarly based on a syncopated motive and using the same leaps of a minor 3rd and minor 6th. But Mozart manipulates these motives much more extensively than Haydn. Bars 95-98 are a slightly modified sequence of bars 91-94. In bars 99-100 a three-note appoggiatura figure is derived from the syncopated motive and treated in half-bar sequences. Tension is maintained as these two bars are themselves treated in a rising sequence in bars 101-102. Another sequence begins in bar 103, but this is cut short when the strings reach the tonic in bar 104. Chromaticism adds to the anguish of this theme (eg the chromatic passing-note at the end of bar 94 and the Neapolitan E♭ in bar 99).

Harmony and tonality: The extract never leaves the tonic key, but the use of chords derived from both versions of the melodic minor and chromatic chords add significantly to the turbulence of the music. As in most classical works, dominant and tonic chords in all inversions prevail, and the rate of change of these chords is slow until the music approaches a cadence. This is evident in the piano solo which begins with a melodically-implied dominant chord (bar 77). For the next eight bars the chords change every two bars (I, IVb, V, I), but as the imperfect cadence approaches the harmony speeds up to one chord per beat (IV^7, II^{7}c, V^{7}b of V, V in bars 86-87). The most notable chromatic chords are the Neapolitan 6th at the start of bar 99 and the secondary dominants in bars 104-105 (eg V^7 of IV on the last beat of bar 104 and the second beat of bar 105). The use of chords derived from the descending melodic minor scale is apparent as the bass ascends in bars 101-104 (consecutive first inversions of chords IV, V, VI, VII and I). At important cadences Mozart reverts to simple tonic-dominant progressions (I, V, I, V, I, II^{7}b, Ic, V, I in bars 88-91 and alternations of tonic and dominant chords in bars 108-114).

Texture: Bars 77-87: The utter simplicity of this three-voice texture disguises the subtlety with which Mozart avoids harmonising the appoggiaturas (there are crotchet rests on the first beat of every even-numbered bar), thus implying rather than stating these dissonances (a feature of Mozartian style which is also apparent in the first four bars of LAM 44).

Bars 88-90: Detached tonic and dominant chords are heard on the piano, the bass of which is underlined by trumpets and timpani. The flute and horns sustain the dominant while oboes conduct a dialogue before the whole windband double the pianist's cadential chords. The whole passage is decorated by the scalic and arpeggio figuration of the piano.

Bars 91-108: The strings were absent in bars 88-90, so now it is their turn to dominate the texture with clearly-defined roles for the upper and lower strings (syncopated figures for the former, menacing scalic figures for the latter). The piano first provides a broken chord accompaniment for the strings, then in bars 99-107 the piano and first violins play heterophonically (the piano part being a decoration of the string melody).

Bars 108-114: Homophonic cadences, first for piano alone, then for piano and windband, finally for the full orchestra.

Form: The extract begins at the first entry of the soloist after an orchestral exposition which includes the first and second subjects, both in the tonic key of D minor. The piano melody is reserved for the soloist, the second exposition beginning at bar 91 with a modified repeat of the first subject, now with the soloist very much in evidence. This double exposition is typical of many sonata-form movements in Mozart's concertos.

LAM 47

Haydn: "Nelson" Mass: Gloria (1798)

Title and text: The day before he was crucified Jesus took bread and wine, blessed them, and gave them to his disciples, bidding them to take and eat them in memory of him. The Mass is the most important of the Christian liturgies. In it the Last Supper is recalled and re-enacted. In a purely musical sense, a mass is a setting of the texts of those parts of the liturgy which remain unaltered in every celebration of the Mass: these are the *Kyrie* (eg LAM 3), the *Gloria* (LAM 47), the *Credo*, the *Sanctus* and *Benedictus* (LAM 71), and the *Agnus Dei* (LAM 95). The *Gloria* is a joyful hymn of praise to God the Father (*Dei Patris*, bars 19-20), God the Son (*Jesu Christe*, bars 14-15), and God the Holy Spirit (*Sancto Spiritu*, bars 17-18). The extract is taken from the last section of the text and includes most of the setting of the final word (*Amen*).

Rhythm: The rushing semiquavers (bars 9-12) and the syncopations (bars 13 and 17-21) in the first violin part serve to underline the joyful nature of the text.

Melody: The melodies are largely diatonic. When accidentals appear they most often propel the music to sharp keys (eg A major in bars 36-37) or they are chromatic sharpenings which resolve upwards (eg the soprano's D♯ in bar 13). Both of these create a bright effect in keeping with the joyful text. In the first part of the extract (bars 9-22) the most important melody is the florid first violin part (the uppermost part of the piano reduction of the orchestral parts). In the fugato (bars 22-49) the melodic interest is divided evenly, each voice part (doubled by strings) singing the triadic and sequential subject (eg sopranos/first violins, bars 33-35[1]) and countersubject (eg bass, bars 24-26[1] also shown in Example 47a). A notable modification of the subject occurs in the soprano part of bars 40-41 where the triadic figures rise sequentially instead of falling. All of the melodic material derives from the subject and countersubject, eg the short, detached motives which are derived by inverting the last few notes of the countersubject (as Examples 47a and 47b show).

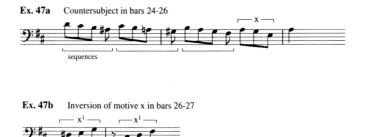

Ex. 47a   Countersubject in bars 24-26

Ex. 47b   Inversion of motive x in bars 26-27

Harmony: As in most classical music Haydn relies heavily on tonic and dominant chords in all inversions. These clearly define the key and drive towards cadences (which often include a cadential 6/4 resolving to chord V). Chords of subdominant function (eg IV and II) are used more sparingly and are sometimes preceded by a secondary dominant. Thus the first phrase (bars 9-10) is harmonised with the following diatonic progression: I, V⁷, I, IIb, II, Ic, V (the last two chords forming an imperfect cadence). In bars 11-15 the progression used in the first two bars is elaborated and extended as follows: V⁷b, I, V⁷d, Ib (repeated in bar 12), IIb, V⁷c of II, IIb, II, Ic, V, I (the last three chords forming a perfect cadence). Above the tonic pedal of bars 15-21 the harmony is similar (eg I, V⁷ of IV, IV, I, IV, V⁷, I changing every minim in bars 15-18). In the fugato (bars 22 to the end) a wider range of chords is used and these are often associated with segments of a circle of fifths used to harmonise the sequential subject and countersubject (as Example 47c shows).

Tonality: Haydn confines himself to closely related keys. The music remains in D major until the Phrygian cadence in B minor in bars 31-32. This key is maintained

Ex. 47c Circle of 5ths underlying the progession in bars 28-29

until the music modulates to A major in bars 36-37, returns to B minor at bar 43, but ends with a perfect cadence in G major.

Texture: This is a symphonic mass, that is to say that the chief focus of interest is the orchestra (the music in this extract would make perfectly good sense without the chorus). In the first six bars there is contrapuntal tension between the first violins' decorated melody and the angular bass part, the other strings providing harmonic filling. The choral parts in this passage are much more chordal, the sopranos presenting a simplification of the first violin part (the two together creating a heterophonic texture above the homophony of the lower voices).

At the other extreme of the textural spectrum is the elaborate counterpoint of the fugato (bar 22 to the end). The texture constantly alternates between two-part counterpoint (eg bars 37-38), three-part counterpoint (eg bars 39-40) and four-part counterpoint (eg bars 48-49). Similar variety is evident in the types of voice-groupings which Haydn deploys, eg basses and orchestral bass instruments in bars 22-23, the lowest three voices in bars 26-27, and the highest three voices in bars 33-34 etc. In the fugal exposition (bars 22-31) each voice announces the subject (starting on A♮) or tonal answer (starting on D♮) in turn, and each of them is accompanied by the regular countersubject shown in Example 47a. A redundant entry is heard in the bass part in bars 30-31. At only two points (the first beats of bars 28 and 30) are all four voices heard together, but the texture becomes busier and often thicker once the key changes and stretti begin at bar 33. This starts with imitative entries of the subject in tenors and sopranos telescoped to an interval of one instead of two bars: the same is true of the altos and sopranos in bars 39-40. In the final stretto of this extract (bars 44-48) the voices enter in quick succession, the tenors imitating the basses after only two beats, the altos entering a bar and a half later, the sopranos a bar after the altos, and the tenors after another bar.

Style and genre: A classical symphonic mass movement.

LAM 49

Beethoven: Fidelio, Act II, Scene 1, No.14 (1805)

Historical context: It is well known that Beethoven at first supported the instigators of the French Revolution with their battle-cry of Freedom, Equality and Brotherhood. But this was not just a political inclination, for he modelled *Fidelio* on the rescue opera of revolutionary France. In particular, he was overwhelmed by the operas of Cherubini who, despite his Italian sounding name, was the greatest of the Parisian dramatic composers, and whose music Beethoven rated above that of any other of his contemporaries. Even here there is a connection with Haydn, for Cherubini's chief claim to fame was his development of truly dramatic operatic ensembles, the continuity of which were guaranteed by symphonic orchestral accompaniments. The source of these ensembles was not Mozart (whose operas were unknown in Paris when Cherubini was writing his first rescue operas), but Haydn's last sets of symphonies, every one of which can be regarded as a miniature opera without words. It is true that there is a direct connection between Mozart's *Magic Flute* and *Fidelio* (both are singspiels and the impresario Schikaneder had a hand in the genesis of both operas). It is also true that Weber's singspiel *Der Freischütz* (LAM 53) carried the development of the genre into the romantic era. But stylistically there is little connection between Act II of *Fidelio* and the Mozartian singspiel on the one hand and the emerging German romantic opera on the other. In many ways *Fidelio* is as much a magnificent full-stop as were Haydn's late masses.

Title: Beethoven's only opera is about married love and its triumph over tyranny. The heroine, Leonora, is married to Florestan who has been unjustly imprisoned. In order to deceive the jailors and gain admission to the prison, she changes her name to Fidelio (the Faithful One) and disguises herself as a young man. Act II is set in the dungeon where one of the jailers (Rocco) and Fidelio are about to dig a grave for Florestan whom the prison governor (Pizzaro) plans to murder to settle an old score. Pizzaro arrives, but before he can carry out his fell purpose Leonora reveals her true identity. The extract begins as Leonora interposes her body between the would-be murderer and her husband. Pizzaro threatens to kill both husband and wife. At this critical juncture a trumpet call announces the arrival of the King's minister who has been sent to end tyranny in this benighted province. Apart from Pizzaro, all, including the other political prisoners, live happily ever after in full enjoyment of the freedom which Leonora's steadfastness has bought for them.

Melody: The furious altercation between the murderer and the saviour is carried on melodic lines of great angularity, Pizzaro's octave leaps being answered by Leonora's leaps of a 7th. But the chief source of musical tension resides in the symphonic orchestral part. Rapid scalic descents are heard in a rising sequence leading to syncopations above another rising sequence in bars 116-125. The trumpet fanfare is, of course, triadic (the only notes that a valveless trumpet can play). All of these melodies contrast with the sense of awe conveyed by the long sustained notes of those about to be rescued (bars 135-141), but Pizzaro 's furious octave leaps are still in evidence as he curses his bad luck.

Harmony and tonality: Beethoven's revolutionary response to his libretto is evident right at the start of the extract where a chord of D major is implied in the first two bars. This is followed by consecutive root position chords of E minor (bars 108-111) and F♯ major (bars 112-113). A tertiary shift returns the music to a chord of D major which is quitted as chord V of G major. In this key a rapid series of perfect cadences is heard (bars 116-119). Just as Beethoven's root position chords rose by step in bars 105-113, so the tonality rises by step – from G major to A minor (bars 119-123), then B minor (bars 123-124) to C major (bar 124). The sequence is cut short by chord V^7 of D major (bars 125-126) and a violent interrupted cadence (ending on the flat submediant, a progression greatly favoured by romantic composers). Beethoven takes this chord of B♭ major as a tonic chord and remains in this key as he slows the rate of change of chords to one chord every two bars (I and Vb in bars 133-136), then one chord per bar (I, IV, Ic, V^7, I in bars 137-141). The tonal stability and primary triads of this section are in stark contrast to the rapidly changing tonality and crude root position triads which accompany Leonora's argument with Pizzaro.

Texture: As in LAM 47, the vocal parts are superimposed on a self-sufficient symphonic argument (both Haydn and Beethoven were first and foremost composers of dramatic instrumental music). This is particularly evident in the final section (bars 133-141) where the principal melody is the triadic line represented by the minims in the right hand part of the piano reduction. This melody sails serenely over the homophonic vocal parts sung by characters who (as the stage direction suggests) seem to be stunned by the orchestral beauty which enfolds them.

Style: As in many of Beethoven's middle-period works the music seems to ride on the very cusp of classicism and romanticism. The triadic melody and functional harmony of bars 133-141 suggest the serene classicism of the late 18th century, but the angular vocal lines and tonal turmoil of the duet mirror the romantic, revolutionary plot. But these are not separate entities thrown together at will. The episode represented in the *Anthology* is the climax of a sonata-form design which begins and ends in D major. In this context the episode in B♭ major is an integral part of a larger formal design and, because the key is so far removed from the sharp keys on either side of it, it also reflects the drama and partakes of the romanticism of the whole of Act II of the opera.

Genre: An ensemble from a revolutionary rescue opera.

LAM 55

Mendelssohn: Octet, Op. 20: 4th Movement (1825)

Title: Is this chamber music? In the sense that it is written for eight solo strings and is usually played by bringing together two established string quartets (whether amateur or professional), it is. But such a large body of instrumentalists would need an unusually large "chamber" in which to play, and Mendelssohn himself said that the work "must be played in a symphonic orchestral style". Both the size of the ensemble and the style in which it should be played suggest that it was written for an audience rather than simply for the sole delectation of the performers.

Rhythm: In the dense contrapuntal textures such as those suggested by the forces Mendelssohn uses, it would be easy to fall into the trap of writing music in which there were simply too many notes. One of the ways Mendelssohn avoids this in the passage printed in the *Anthology* is to contrast a theme consisting solely of rushing quavers with themes consisting of minims or semibreves and minims (this is very obvious in the first few bars of the extract where the rhythms of the first violin and first viola are sharply contrasted). Even when two or three instrumentalists play the quaver theme together, there is no lack of clarity because they are playing, not contrapuntally, but in parallel thirds or sixths with each other and so are heard as a single thematic block standing out against the other instruments playing longer notes. Because of the extremely fast tempo (presto in 2/2 time), clear textures are essential in this movement.

Ex. 55   Bars 255-263 of Mendelssohn's Octet

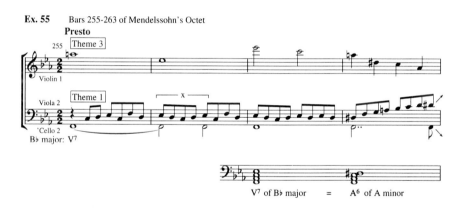

Melody: Example 55 shows the three principal themes of this extract. Theme 1 is a largely conjunct moto perpetuo which snakes its way from one instrument to another throughout most of this passage. It contrasts with the triadic theme 3 which, at this point, outlines a diminished chord (or a dominant 7th if the bass F♮ is added). In bar 259 of Example 55 Mendelssohn's E♭s have been enharmonically renotated as D♯s in both themes (the reason for this will become apparent later). Theme 2 begins triadically but ends with a conjunct figure (z) which derives from one of the motives in theme 1 (compare the second viola part in bars 259-260 with the first violin part in bars 262-263).

These three themes are constantly modified and their motives manipulated to fit the changing contrapuntal and harmonic contexts. For instance, at the start of the extract all three motives (x, y and z) shown in the viola parts of Example 55 are heard in the first violin part, starting with sequences of y (bars 213-215^1), then a free inversion of x (the first five notes of bar 216), and finally z in the major (bars 217^2-218^1). The beginning and end of theme 2 (Example 55) are changed (viola 1, bars 213-217^1) to form a fugal subject which is almost the same as Handel's fugal subject in the "Halleluia Chorus" (*And he shall reign for ever and ever*). When theme 3 is first heard in this extract (first violin, bars 243-246) it outlines a major triad (rather than the diminished triad outlined in Example 55).

Texture: Mendelssohn deploys his themes and free parts in a dazzling array of textures, beginning fugally (theme 2 being the subject and theme 1 the countersubject in this extract), and ending with two-part counterpoint supported by chords (bars 243-263). Some idea of the variety of these textures may be gained from the following descriptive analysis which aims to identify the principal themes in their contrapuntal contexts.

Bars 213-217^1: Two-part counterpoint between viola 1 (subject/theme 2) and violin 1 (countersubject/theme 1).
Bars 217^2-221^1: Three-part counterpoint in which the subject (violin 2) and countersubject (viola 2) are contrapuntally combined with a free part (viola 1).
Bars 221^2-225^1: Four-part counterpoint with the countersubject played by the first viola and the subject played in octaves by the cellos (the other two parts being free).
Bars 225^2-229^1: Four and five-part counterpoint in which the end of theme 2 (subject) reverts to the form it takes in Example 55. This overlaps with:
Bars 228^2-233^1: Four and five-part counterpoint in which abridged forms of the subject are heard in stretto on violin 3, violin 4, cello 2 and violin 1 (in that order) while the second violin continues with the countersubject.
Bars 233^2-242: The last of the stretto entries (violin 1, bars 232-233) only got as far as the initial rising perfect 4th of theme 2. In this section Mendelssohn takes this opening as the start of a new variant of theme 2 treated canonically between violin 3 and the cellos (still in octaves) while violins 1 and 2 and viola 1 continue the countersubject in parallel 6/3 chords.
Bars 243-258: This passage falls into four 4-bar phrases, each of them containing theme 3 (violin 1, violin 2, violin 3, then violin 1 again) contrapuntally combined with theme 1 (violin 4, violin 3, viola 1 and viola 2). This two-part counterpoint is supported by the homophony of the other instruments. In these bars double-stopping sometimes produces chords of up to 10 parts (excluding doubling at the unison).
Bars 259-263: Theme 2 is played by all of the violins with theme 1 on violas and a functional bass provided by the cellos (still in octaves).

Harmony and tonality: On page 210 keys are defined more by the principal melodies than by the harmonic progressions. The fugal subject is thus heard flashing by in E$\flat$ major (bars 213-217), G minor (bars 217-221), C minor (bars 221-225), F minor (225-229) and E$\flat$ major modulating to A$\flat$ major (bars 230-233). Tonality becomes stable in bars 233-237 where the canon outlines the tonic chord of A$\flat$ major. In bars 238-242 the dominant 7th chords of B$\flat$ major and C minor are both decorated with bass appoggiaturas. This is followed by a perfect cadence in C minor (bars 240-241) and a Phrygian cadence in D minor (bars 242-243). Over the same bass note chord V of D minor (bars 243-246) changes to the dominant minor 9th chord of G minor (bars 247-250). This diminished 7th chord is quitted as V^{m9} of V in C major when it resolves on to chord Ic in this key at bar 251. Example 55 shows how the next chord (V^7 in B$\flat$ major) is quitted as a chord of the augmented 6th when it resolves on to chord Ic of A minor (in Example 55 bar 258 has been re-notated to show how the E$\flat$ of the dominant 7th chord effectively becomes a D$\sharp$, resolving up a step to the dominant of A minor, while the bass resolves down a step to the same note). The extract ends with the only straightforward diatonic harmony in the whole of this tumultuous passage (analysed in Example 55).

Formal context: The extract is taken from a sonata-form movement which incorporates fugal textures. The movement starts in the tonic key of E$\flat$ major with Theme 1 (Example 55) which is the subject of a fugato. Themes 2 and 3 are both contrapuntally combined with theme 1 in the exposition. LAM 55 is part of the development section of this finale.

LAM 62

Schumann: Piano Quintet Op.44: 1st Movement (1842)

Title: Mozart wrote a quintet for piano and winds (LAM 43), but Schumann was the first to write a quintet for piano and string quartet.

Rhythm: The most pervasive rhythm is that of the accompaniment (weak-strong-weak in 2/2 time). More startling is the syncopation in bars 103-104: this is a Schumannesque fingerprint in which the syncopation is not caused by weak-beat or off-beat accentuation, but by replacing the strong beats with silences.

Melody: It is easy to miss the structure of Schumann's lovely second subject theme (bars 79-95) when one is lost in admiration for its seemingly effortless lyricism. It begins with a two-bar phrase characterised by a downward leap and a scalic ascent (cello, bars 79-80). A chromatic passing note (F♯) links this question to its poetic answer as the melodic line moves to the viola. The answer comes in the form of an inversion of the question (see Example 62a). This overlaps a sequential repetition of all four bars (notice that, because the phrase is now in the minor, the chromatic passing note comes half a beat earlier than in bar 80). The cello begins the question for a third time (bar 87), but the scale turns into an arpeggio, reaching a note (bar 89) a perfect 5th higher than it would have done had the sequence continued. But this is not the end of the phrase, for the cello continues to rise to the climax of the theme, the top A♮ in bar 91. The descent is achieved by using modified fragments of the question: first a downward leap of an octave (instead of the 5th in bar 79) followed by the dotted-note figure (compare y in Example 62a with y¹ in Example 62b), then motive z sequentially repeated to reach the tonic of F major in bar 95). The lengthening of the last note in motive y¹ (Example 62b) allows the first violin (doubled at the octave below by the viola) to join the conversation by interposing motive z. The first violin's cadence is formed from motive y, as y¹ in Example 62b shows.

Ex. 62a

Ex. 62b

Harmony and tonality: The extract begins with a perfect cadence in F major (Ic V⁷ I) played by the strings. But Schumann skilfully grafts the piano's chord of VII⁷ of B♭ major (piano, bar 73) on top of the strings' chord of F major, thus turning the tonic chord of F major into the complete dominant major 9th chord of B♭ major. Such harmonic subtlety is another Schumannesque fingerprint. This chord accompanies a pre-echo of motive x (Example 62a) with an elongated chromatic passing-note (F♯) and an appoggiatura in the bass (B♭): both resolve back to the outer notes of chord VII⁷. Eventually the chord resolves to the tonic in bar 79.

The diatonic progression in this key (I, VIb, II⁷, VIIb, III in bars 79-88, each chord lasting two bars) is typically romantic in its use of secondary triads (compare this progression with Haydn's use of tonic and dominant chords in bars 9-15 of LAM 47). The secondary dominant (V^{m9} of III) on the second beat of bar 88 is equally romantic: it emphasises the minor hue of chord III and clashes gently with the cello D♮. This D minor chord is quitted as chord VI in F major: it is followed by V^7c of V (bar 90) and alternations of chords Ic and V^7 (bars 91-94). The cadence is similar to that already described at the start of the extract (ie a perfect cadence in F major turned back towards B♭ major by the piano chord). But there is one telling difference. If Example 62b is played without the other instruments the parallel 4ths between the violin and cello at the cadence will sound very harsh. The reason they sound no more than pleasantly dissonant is that each part is decorating the dominant chord, the violin with an échappé which resolves by leap to the tonic, and the cello with an appoggiatura which resolves by step to the leading-note (a similar situation is brought about when parallel 5ths occur at cadences in Bach's chorale harmonisations: the result of a passing 7th in the dominant chord moving at the same time as an anticipation).

Instead of the expected tonic chord of B♭ major in bar 99 a chord of G♭ major in first inversion is built up one note at a time. This is, in fact, part of an inverted interrupted cadence in B♭ major (ie chord V and chord VI on the flat submediant, both chords in first inversion). To this G♭ major triad Schumann adds an augmented 6th (the E♮ on the first beat of bar 102) which, instead of resolving, remains in chord V^7c of V on the next beat. This secondary dominant resolves irregularly onto the complete dominant major 9th of B♭ major (again!). The final chord of the extract is another secondary dominant (V^7 of VI) but it makes little sense without the cadence which, alas, does not follow it in this extract!

Taking a satellite's view of the whole extract it can be seen that underlying the chromatic complexities of the harmony there is a very simple tonal structure. Disregarding the first eight bars (which belong to the previous section and which are repeated with only minor changes in bars 93-98) the music begins in B♭ major, modulates to its dominant (F major) in bars 91-95 and returns whence it came in the remainder of the extract.

Texture: Schumann's chamber music with piano is sometimes criticised by those who have not played it, for favouring the piano at the expense of the strings . This extract gives the lie to that notion. The principal melodic line at the start is given to the cello, with the other instruments providing a homophonic accompaniment. The piano takes the lead in bars 73-78 and 95-98 where the strings simply underline the piano chords. But in bars 79-94 it is the turn of the piano to provide a chordal accompaniment for the cello and viola love-duet (with sighing appoggiaturas from the first violin) and for the more passionate conversation of the cello and first violin shown in Example 62b. Only the second violin plays the part of a wall-flower at the ball.

Formal context: The extract is taken from the second subject in the exposition of a sonata-form movement in E♭ major. Hence the prevailing key is the dominant, B♭ major.

LAM 67

Liszt: Concert Paraphrase of Rigoletto (1859)

Title: In the sense in which Liszt used the term, a paraphrase was an attempt to reproduce the essence of vocal or orchestral music in a keyboard idiom. In this case LAM 67 is an operatic paraphrase of Verdi's opera *Rigoletto* (LAM 66). The Lisztian paraphrase was no mere transcription (like the piano reduction of LAM 47), it was a thorough reworking of the original in which pianistic figuration might be added (such as the notes printed in small type in LAM 67), melody and harmony changed (compare bar 63 of Example 67a with bar 26 of Example 67b), and new material interpolated (eg bars 66-68 of LAM 67). One of the reasons for these changes is that the piano is incapable of the vocal nuances with which good singers can suggest the tenderness, passion or anger of dramatic characters. In the absence of timbral variation and dynamic change on a single note, the pianist must rely on elements such as dissonance or chromaticism to suggest these changing moods.

The word "concert" suggests that this was a major piano piece designed, not for amateur performance at home, but for virtuosic display in a public recital.

Ex. 67 Verdi's Rigoletto and Liszt's Concert Paraphrase compared

Melody: Example 67a shows the melody and harmony of bars 60-64 of LAM 66. It is entirely diatonic apart from a chromatic passing-note (G♮ in bar 62). Example 67b shows a passage from the Paraphrase which is not included in LAM 67. In it Liszt introduces another and very telling chromaticism: instead of the vocal perfect 5ths (bar 63 of LAM 66 and Example 67a), Liszt colours the melodic line by introducing a tritone (the notorious *diabolus in musica*) to suggest the duplicity of the Duke. The corresponding passage in LAM 67 is shown in Example 67c. In these bars (62-65) the tritone has been augmented by an octave then, in bar 66 (the start of a Lisztian interpolation) the interval becomes a compound perfect 5th.

The cadence figure (z in Example 67a) is reproduced unchanged earlier in the Paraphrase (compare Examples 67a and 67b), but in the corresponding passage in LAM 67 the cadence figure (z^1 in Example 67c) is shorn of the tonic and is replaced by a dramatic pause. In bar 66 the cadence figure (z^2 in Example 67c) is transposed up a semitone and cadences appear, not on the tonic, but on the mediant of D♭ major (ie the F♮ in bar 67). There is a prolongation of the perfect cadence in bars 67 and 68 (represented by two chords in Example 67c) which delays the arrival of the cadence figure (z^3, which reproduces the pitches, but not the rhythm of Verdi's original) and the clinching perfect cadence in D♭ major.

In LAM 67 Maddalena's flirtatious staccato melody is reproduced unchanged in bar 60 (which corresponds with bar 64 of LAM 66), but the dominant harmony which Liszt uses in bar 62 entails some slight melodic modification to fit the new chord (compare bar 66 of LAM 66 with bar 62 of LAM 67).

Harmony and tonality: Though very chromatic, Liszt remains within the key of D♭ major throughout LAM 67, the apparent dominant 7th of D major in bar 66 being an enharmonic notation of the chord of the augmented 6th of D♭ major (the E♯ accidental in the chord on the first beat of this bar is a misprint – it should be a ♮ like that on the second beat). The tonic key is firmly established in bars 59-63 by diatonic harmony (I, I, Ib, V^7c, Ib in bars 59, 60, 61 and 62 respectively). After this Liszt goes his own way, as Example 67c shows.

In bar 63 a secondary dominant (V7b of IV in Example 67c) replaces the original repetition of chord Ib. Instead of resolving to chord IV Liszt raises the D♭ by a semitone to change the original secondary dominant to a diminished 7th chord (V^{m9} of II in bar 64 of Example 67c). This is suspended over the 3rd of chord IIb, a chord which is implied by the bass G♭ and realised when the diminished 7th resolves completely on the third beat of bar 64. Chord ii^{7}b in bar 65 is borrowed from the tonic minor (D♭ minor: an enharmonic notation of the chord in C♯ minor is shown below bar 65 in Example 67c).

The German augmented 6th of D♭ major (or minor) is constructed on the flat submediant, B♭♭. It consists of this note (the root) plus a major 3rd above it (D♭), a perfect 5th above it (F♭) and an augmented 6th above it (G♮). The augmented 6th (G♮) resolves up a semitone to the dominant (A♭), and the root resolves down a semitone to the lower dominant (as shown on the stave below bars 66-67 in Example 67c). After the resolution to chord Ic at the start of bar 67, the left hand chords are V^{m9} of II, iic (again borrowed from the tonic minor) and V^{m9} of III, all of them over a dominant pedal. At least this is what the progression appears to be on paper. The aural phenomenon is simply that of chord Ic (bar 67 in Example 67c) resolving to the complete dominant major 9th chord (bar 68 in Example 67c) leading to a perfect cadence (bars 68-69 in Example 67c) with a kaleidoscope of chromatic coruscations between each chord.

Piano textures: Liszt divides the Duke's melody between fingers 1, 2 and 3 of each hand in the tenor register of the piano. This allows the other fingers of the left hand to provide harmonic support and the right hand to decorate the operatic music with pianistic arabesques. Maddalena's scoffing laughter is represented by tinkling octaves in the highest register of the keyboard while the left hand provides both harmonic support and a continuation of the delicate arabesques. In bars 65 and 67 the melody is embellished with chromatic scales reaching a one-handed double trill (bar 66) then a broken diminished 7th chord (bar 67) which includes the highest note in this extract (a G♮ which is only a perfect 4th below the highest note of a modern grand piano). In bar 68 the dominant major ninth chord is spread over four octaves with the help of the sustaining pedal. This is followed by typical Lisztian chromatic bedazzlement (the right hand outlines the major 9th chord in the rapid descent on the last stave of LAM 67 while the left hand provides a variety of chromatic embellishments). Only in the last couple of beats do we hear unadorned chords supporting the original cadence figure (z in

Example 67). In this short extract alone Liszt showers over six octaves of the keyboard with an amazing array of virtuoso figuration and textures.

Style and genre: A romantic operatic paraphrase. With the advent of recordings in the 20th century, the need for piano transcriptions and paraphrases of orchestral and vocal music died out. Only now, 150 years after Liszt wrote this music, is an appreciation of the best examples of the genre beginning to re-emerge.

LAM 68

Wagner: Concert Prelude: Tristan und Isolde (1859)

Title: Wagner's music drama, *Tristan and Isolde*, is about the forbidden love of Isolde for Tristan who has been sent by King Mark to bring Isolde, his intended bride, from Ireland to his Cornish kingdom. Tristan reciprocates Isolde's love, but he denies himself any outward expression until they both inadvertently drink a love potion and fall into each others arms before they disembark and meet Isolde's intended husband. The second act is set in the garden of King Mark's castle in Cornwall. It is largely taken up with a meeting of the lovers while the King is out hunting. "Tristan draws Isolde gently down on a flowery bank ... sinks on his knees before her and rests his head on her arm" (Wagner's stage direction). In this position they sing a passionate duet until they are surprised by King Mark and his retinue. The King laments Tristan's disloyalty. One of the knights lunges at Tristan who, making no effort to defend himself, is mortally wounded. The third act is set in Tristan's castle in Brittany whither he has been carried to die. Only Isolde can heal his wounds. When, in his delirium, Tristan receives news that she has come, he tears off his bandages and dies in her arms. After singing the famous *Liebestod* (Love-death), Isolde "as if glorified" sinks down upon Tristan's body and expires. Though not represented in the opera, the legend has it that King Mark, forgiving them both, has them buried next to each other. Over one of the graves grows an ivy, over the other a vine, the two plants inseparably entwined.

Up to bar 92 the *Concert Prelude* is exactly the same as the operatic prelude, which, after this point, modulates to the dominant of C minor and flows straight into the opera itself. Because of the exorbitant demands they made, Wagner's later operas could not be staged until the composer could find a rich patron (King Ludwig II of Bavaria eventually provided the wherewithal). Meanwhile Wagner needed cash badly. One of his solutions was to provide the operatic prelude with a new ending so the whole *Concert Prelude* would make good musical sense as an independent instrumental work. The *Concert Prelude* could then immediately be performed and thus yield a handsome profit. So Wagner added a new ending (bars 93-118) to his already-written operatic prelude. For this he used material from Act II and the end of the opera, transposed to fit the home key of the Prelude, A minor/major (Romantic composers slipped from the tonic minor to the tonic major and back as a matter of course). Thus, beginning in A minor and ending in A major, the *Concert Prelude* makes complete tonal sense as a self-standing orchestral work.

It also makes good sense in terms of the programme Wagner wrote for its first performance. He says that the *Concert Prelude* rises from "insatiable longing ... through anxious sighs ... to the mightiest onset ... of love's endless rapture ... [before] the heart sinks back to languish in longing ... until in final exhaustion ... [it] catches a glimmer of highest rapture ... of dying ... of final redemption". The "insatiable longing" is represented by motive x (the so-called Desire Motive shown in Example 68a) which rises sequentially to the first "anxious sigh" (the appoggiatura over chord VI in the interrupted cadence of bars 16-17). The "mightiest onset of love's endless rapture" is clearly the final climax of the Prelude at bar 83, while the heart "sinking back to languish in longing" is the descent from this unresolved climax (bars 84-92). The concert ending is a reworking of the music from Act II, scene 2 that accompanies the lovers as they sink upon the flowery bank (bars 93-101 in Example 68a) plus a reworking of Isolde's *Liebestod* (bars 101-118 in Example 68a). It will be seen that in his reworking of these final bars of the opera, Wagner features alternating woodwind and string phrases – symbols of the ivy and vine which are themselves symbols of Tristan and Isolde's undying love.

Melody and motive: Two aspects of Wagner's melodic writing in his mature works are of vital importance. The most obvious is his use of short memorable motives which, by association with particular words or phrases of the libretto, come to signify those words or phrases whenever they are repeated. It is because of this association that motive x in Example 68a has been called the "Desire Motive" and motive y the "Grief Motive". While such names work fairly well in much of *The Ring* (a cycle of four operas which Wagner was working on when he began work on "Tristan") they can be confusing as references in the *Concert Prelude* for the following reasons: they cannot be associated with particular words or phrases by those who have not previously heard the whole opera, different commentators ascribe different names to the same musical motive, and in Tristan the motives are constantly mutating to form part of a longer melody.

Less obvious is this longer melody itself. Wagner called it "unending melody". It is like a thread running throughout the *Concert Prelude*, a thread which is quite obvious to the ear, but which is difficult to extricate from the polyphony of the full score. The unending melody of the whole *Concert Prelude* is represented in Example 68a (together with some other contrapuntal voices when they are of equal importance). The analysis which follows refers exclusively to this Example.

Nearly every note of the unending melody derives from just three motives, and these three motives are used as the building blocks of three themes:

> **x** – a rising chromatic scale (some call it the "Desire Motive") first heard in bars 2-3,
>
> **y** – a rising 6th and a falling semitone (the "Grief Motive") heard right at the start of the Prelude,
>
> **z** – a five-note diatonic figure (the "Glance Motive") first heard in bars 17-18 which itself falls into two smaller motives, a three-note dotted-rhythm figure encompassing a rising third (a) and a two-note falling figure (b).

Ex. 68a

Theme 1 (bars 1-17)

The Prelude begins with motive y on the cellos (Vc) answered by motive x on an oboe (Ob). Even at the very start however, the motives begin to mutate, for motive y actually continues for nearly two bars more in the English horn part (EH). The cellos' falling semitone in bar 1 together with this continuation forms an inversion of motive x (xI = x melodically inverted). These motives are heard again in the exact sequence of bars 4-7 (Cl = clarinet). In bars 8-11 Wagner extends both motives by one note (x^1 and y^1). In the process the cellos play an exact retrograde of the version of x heard in bars 2-3 (xR = x backwards). After a repeat of bars 10-11 (Fl = flute), and after twice echoing the last two notes of x^1 (vln = violins and ww = woodwind), Wagner concludes his first theme by interpolating an appoggiatura (B♮) between the last two notes of x^1 (bars 16-17) to form another variant (x^2). The resolution of the appoggiatura overlaps with the next theme. The effect of theme 1 is, in large measure, dependent upon the use of silence, so, in a literal sense, it is not "unending". To see how Wagner can make a continuous melody from motive x we need to look at the recapitulation (bars 68-74) where x, x^1 and x^2 are telescoped to form a seven-bar melody (which continues as a countermelody to the second theme).

Theme 2 (bars 17-24)

This begins with three mutations of the third and last motive, z. In z^1 figure a remains unchanged (apart from the transposition up a 3rd), but figure b becomes an appoggiatura figure. In z^2 the rhythm of figure a is slightly altered by the tie, while figure b (a falling 7th) is melodically inverted to a rising 7th (bI = b melodically inverted). From this point on Wagner manipulates figures a and b as separate entities starting with two inversions of a (bars 20-21). The motive in the second half of bar 21 shows how Wagner can combine elements of two motives to form new offspring (a^2 has the rhythm of figure a and the on-beat falling step of figure b^1). A similar process is at work in the first half of bar 22 where figure b^1 is combined with a rhythmic diminution of an inversion of the falling 7th of figure b. The theme ends with chromatic scales which can be seen as versions of figure a (shown by the stems and beams below the stave) decorated with chromatic passing-notes and ending with an inversion of b^1, but it is equally possible to hear them as rhythmically-altered versions of motive x and x^1.

Theme 3 (bars 25-32^3)

This apparently new theme is in fact constructed from figures a and b from motive z in Theme 2. It is amazing how different motive z sounds when figures a and b are reversed in the viola part (Vla) of bar 25. Another apparently new motive (which some call the "Poison" or "Death" motive) is heard in the double basses (Cb) in bars 28-29 and 30-31. In fact this is another retrograde (yR = y backwards).

These then are the three motives and the three themes which are built from them. In the remainder of Example 68a the derivations of motives are not shown where Wagner exactly repeats a previous section (eg bars 32^4-36^3). It will not be necessary to comment on all of the motives which have been labelled (the label itself being sufficient explanation), but it would be as well to examine new manipulations. For instance in bar 44 Wagner rhythmically augments figure b^1 (b^{1}A), but this happens over an interrupted cadence very similar to that in bars 16-17, so instead of regarding the melody in bars 43-44 as an agglomeration of motives x, a^4 (see bar 29) and b^{1}A, one can regard the whole passage as a variant of x^2. As the biggest climax approaches, a triadic version of figure a is heard in conjunction with the inversion of b^1 (bars 63-64). Together they form another variant of motive z (z^4 in bars 64-65) which is heard in a rising sequence. The ascending scales which precede every statement of z^4 do not derive from any of the three motives: they were a late, and very effective addition to the score (as Wagner's Preliminary Draft shows). Wagner builds to the last and greatest climax (bar 83) by contrapuntally combining all three motives in bars 81-82.

The concert ending forms a coda in which Wagner quotes from the love scene in Act II (bars 93-98, which include a repeat of the second half of the phrase). This is directly linked to a quotation from the end of the opera (bars 101-113). It will be seen that the motive in these final bars (which some call "Love's Bliss") is an abridged version of the violin melody in bars 98-101, but it is also another version of the cadential motive x^2 first heard in bars 16-17 (with the same appoggiatura above an interrupted cadence). Bars 101-113 are entirely devoted to a dialogue (ivy and vine) based on variants of this motive. But after the appoggiatura and its resolution (B♮-A♮) in bar 113 the melodic line reverses direction and slowly rises to reach the 5th of the final tonic chord. Meanwhile the oboes and English horn enter with a final statement of motive x^1 which is extended to resolve onto the major 3rd of the final tonic chord.

Harmony and tonality: Wagner disguises the functional skeleton of his harmonic progressions with so many dissonances and chromaticisms (both melodic and harmonic) that it is sometimes almost impossible to analyse his chords in relation to a specific key (though we can instinctively recognise the tonality in almost every bar of the Prelude).

This is the case in his harmonisation of theme 1 (bars 1-17). The chord of the augmented 6th in its so-called German form consists of a major triad on the flat submediant together with a note an augmented 6th above the root. This is the chord in bar 258 of Example 55 (ie chord VI of A minor with a D♯ added). As is perfectly normal this German 6th resolves onto chord Ic. Another version of the augmented 6th chord is the French 6th. Like the German 6th it comprises the root (the flat submediant) and a major 3rd and augmented 6th above it. However the perfect 5th is replaced by an augmented 4th above the root (the B♮ in the first bar of Example 68b). Like Mendelssohn's music in bars 258-263 of Example 55, the opening of the Prelude is in A minor, but Wagner disguises the French 6th chord with a long-held appoggiatura: this is the famous Tristan chord which recurs throughout most of the Prelude (see Example 68b). The appoggiatura resolves to the 3rd of the French 6th (A♮) on the last quaver of bar 2. When the French 6th resolves onto V^7 Wagner disguises it with the chromatic passing-note A♯ (cpn in Example 68b), but this soon resolves to the 5th of the dominant chord. However the dominant 7th chord itself does not resolve to chord I (as Mendelssohn's does at the end of Example 55).

It might be asked how we can assume the music to be in A minor if the tonic chord is absent. There are many factors which contribute to our perception of this key. In tonal music we have for centuries been conditioned to at least attempt to ascribe a tonal centre to the music we hear (whether consciously or unconsciously). This is the case at the start of the Prelude. At a very slow tempo we first hear an A♮ and this is followed by a leap up to an F♮. Of itself the leap creates a sense of dissonance which requires the resolution it achieves as it falls a semitone. So this figure comprises a decoration of a perfect 5th suggesting the root and 5th of a tonic triad in A minor (not A major, since this key does not contain an F♮). If a scale is constructed from all of the notes played in bars 0-5 this will be the result: A, (A♯), B, [C♮] D, (D♯), E, F, G, G♯, A.

Ex. 68b

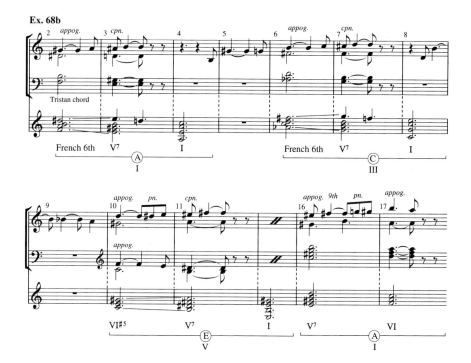

Apart from the two notes in round brackets, all of these notes can be found in the scales of A minor (harmonic, and ascending and descending melodic). Both the A♯ and the D♯ resolve by step to a diatonic note in chord V⁷, so they are perceived as chromatic decorations. The only note of the scale to be omitted is the minor 3rd (the C♮ in square brackets), but, as we have already noted, the presence of an F♮ precludes the possibility of A major. Finally, any dominant 7th chord of itself implies a resolution to its tonic (which is why Mendelssohn's re-interpretation of the dominant 7th chord of B♭ major as the augmented 6th chord of A minor creates such a pleasant surprise in Example 55).

Example 68b shows that the music of bars 6-7 of the Prelude is an exact sequence of bars 3-4 in C. In bars 10-11 however he subtly varies the progression. Instead of a French 6th he uses an augmented triad on the flat submediant in the key of E . This chord functions in the same way as the French 6th did (ie the outer notes need to resolve by a semitone in contrary motion – G♯ up to A and C♮ down to B♮), and like the two previous progressions the resolution is to a dominant 7th (in this case in the key of E). As in the previous progressions these chords are disguised by dissonant and chromatic decorations. In the treble, a dissonant appoggiatura resolves upwards to the consonant 3rd of the augmented triad by way of a passing-note (pn). The dissonant F♮ in the tenor resolves directly to the same note. As in the other two progressions, chord V⁷ is decorated with a chromatic passing-note (E♯).

After repetitions of parts of this progression, Wagner, in bars 16-17, adds a minor 7th to the implied tonic chord of E major, thus returning to the tonality of the opening bars (A minor). Above this chord a chromatic appoggiatura half resolves to an F♯ (a major 9th above the root) which itself resolves to the consonant G♯ by way of a passing-note. The second chord of this interrupted cadence is also decorated with an appoggiatura (very telling because the G♯ is the leading-note which we expect to rise a semitone to the tonic).

If we now leave the trees to examine the whole wood we will see that Wagner has started in A minor then modulated through the keys of C and E back to A minor. Added together, the tonic notes of these keys make chord I of A minor (shown by the encircled letters which stand for keys in Example 68b). Indeed one could see this entire passage as an elaboration of chords I, III, V and I again in the key of A minor.

The harmonisation of Theme 1 illustrates a number of features which are characteristic of Wagner's progressions throughout the Prelude:
• keys are often implied rather than stated,
• the mode of keys (major or minor) is sometimes ambiguous or changes rapidly,
• dissonant chords are often left unresolved or resolve irregularly,
• changes of key are often tertiary (A minor, up a third to C major, up a third to E major),

- chromatic chords such as the French 6th are used freely,
- melodic dissonances and chromaticisms occur frequently, often obscuring the underlying progressions.

A complete tonal analysis would be impossible in a book of this length, but it is necessary to point out the chief tonal centres to enable the structure of the Prelude to be clarified. These tonal centres are most apparent in Wagner's cadences (though on-going polyphony superficially obscures most of them). In Example 68a these cadences are shown by brackets enclosing an encircled capital letter. We have already noticed how the interrupted cadence of bars 16-17 clinches the key of A minor. Similarly the perfect cadence in bar 24 confirms the key of A major.

Although there is no cadence to confirm it, bars 25-28 are clearly in E major, but by bars 35-36 and 43-44 there are more interrupted cadences, the first in F major, the second in C♯ minor. With the return of theme 3 starting at bar 45 comes a return to E major. The long, decorated dominant pedal in bars 63-69 suggests the return of A major/minor, but this expectation is defeated when the Tristan chord returns in bar 70 (A flat, B♮, D♮ and F♯) resolving on to V^7 of C in the next bar, then the same progression in A (bars 72-73) which leads to a restatement of the original interrupted cadence of bars 16-17 in bars 73-74. This fails to re-establish the key of A minor, instead the music veers off to C major (emphasised by the timpani pedal in bars 74-77). The Tristan chord, resolving to a dominant 7th, is then repeated several times in B♭ flat major/minor (bars 77-78) then E♭ major/minor (bars 79-83). In this key the original Tristan chord (enharmonically notated as F, A♭, C♭ and E♭) is heard at the greatest climax of the piece (bar 83). It fails to resolve in the key of E♭ major/minor, instead the original notation returns and the Tristan chord resolves onto V^7 in A minor as at the start of the Prelude (bars 83-84). The original sequence is maintained as the Tristan chord resolves onto V^7 of C major in bars 86-87, but the next Tristan chord resolves to V^7 of D major/minor via an augmented 6th chord in bars 89-90. In bars 90-91 and 91-92 augmented 6th chords replace the Tristan chords as they resolve to V^7 of F major/minor and G major/minor respectively.

Finally the goal of A major is achieved by the progression shown in bars 92-95 in Example 68a (but even now there is no perfect cadence, instead there is an unusual interrupted cadence consisting of chords V^7 and IV). The rest of the coda remains firmly in the tonic key of A major. From bar 102-109 three plagal cadences are heard, then, over a tonic pedal, V^7 and I alternate (bars 109-113). Finally the Tristan chord (bar 114) resolves to minor chord IV (bar 115, still over the tonic pedal) which itself resolves to an unalloyed tonic chord.

Instrumentation and orchestral textures: Wagner demands a large orchestra which, as page 259 shows, comprises:

3 Fl.: three flutes

Hb.: two oboes

Cl.: two clarinets in A (sounding a minor third lower than the printed pitches)

EH.: English horn or cor anglais (sounding a perfect fifth lower than the printed pitches)

4 Hr.1.(F) and 2.(F): six horns in F (sounding a perfect fifth lower than the printed pitches)

3.(E) and 4.(E): seven horns in E (sounding a minor sixth lower than the printed pitches)

3 Fg: three bassoons

Bcl: bass clarinet in A (sounding a minor third lower than the printed pitches, whether in bass or treble clef in German notation)

2 Trompeten (F): two trumpets in F (sounding a perfect fourth above the printed pitches)

3 Pos.: three trombones (two tenor and one bass)

Btb.: bass tuba

Pk.: three timpani tuned to C, E and F

Vl.: first and second violins

Br.: violas

Vc.: cellos

Cb.: double basses (sounding an octave lower than printed)

The harp (Harfe) does not enter until the coda (bar 95).

Wagner treats these forces with great restraint, delaying the entry of the heavy brass and drums until the lead up to the final climax: the trombones enter for the first time in bar 66, the tuba and drums in bar 74, the trumpets in bar 81 (they play no more than nine notes in the whole Prelude). Wagner tends to use his instruments in groups or in layers, contrasting music in low, middle and high registers. Thus the first 13 bars are scored for cellos and woodwind only (apart from one horn note), and he contrasts the middle register of the first 11 bars with the high register after the first pause. After the second pause, violins in octaves in the middle register are contrasted with woodwind octaves in a higher register. The structurally important interrupted cadence in bars 16-17 involves most of the orchestra apart from the heavy brass and drums, with the dominant 7th chord played pizzicato and chord VI bowed (Bog. = Bogen or arco).

Theme 2 (bars 17-24) is given to middle-register cellos supported by low-register woodwind and pizzicato violas and basses. It then passes to the second then first violins (both playing on their G strings) supported by bass clarinet and lower strings.

With the entry of the theme 3 (bars 25-32, violas, doubled at the octave above by first violins in the second half) the texture becomes increasingly contrapuntal as the retrograde of y enters on bassoons and double basses.

The repeat of the theme 2 (bars 32-36) is rescored for woodwind with motive x extended by second violins and violas.

In bars 36-42 low strings and high woodwind exchange motive z antiphonally.

The build up to the greatest climax begins after the string cadence in bars 43-44. From this point on the texture is layered, woodwind in octaves taking theme 3 and a sequential development of motive z (bars 45-54) while bass instruments play the retrograde of y and motive x in augmentation, the other instruments having free contrapuntal parts. The end of this woodwind layer overlaps with a repeat of the first four bars of theme 2 (bars 55-58) played in octaves by first violins and cellos while the basses play another augmentation of motive x and the inner strings play a syncopated version of the same motive. In bars 58-63 theme 2 starts again in a woodwind layer against a continuing descending chromatic layer on first violins and cellos.

In bars 63-73 motive z^4 and its scalic prefix is passed imitatively between string sections, then, as the recapitulation gets underway in upper woodwind and horns, all strings except for the double basses play motive z^4 and versions of the prefix. This overlaps with a repeat of theme 2 in string octaves (bars 74-77) and a development of the cadence figure (bars 77-81). The entry of the trumpets (motive x in bars 81-82) coincides with the most complex counterpoint in the Prelude. There are four distinct layers:
 • versions of motive z on upper woodwind,
 • repetitions of motive y on horns, bass clarinet, violas (tremolo) and cellos,
 • motive x on trumpets,
 • a return of the scalic prefix on violins.

After the tutti climax (bar 83) there is a rapid withdrawal of brass and drums followed by antiphonal exchanges of motives z (violins), y (lower strings), and x (upper woodwind).

Motives z^2 and x^1 on violas (bars 92-94) playing above the other strings (including the violins), link the operatic prelude to the coda, the melodic line passing seamlessly to a solo oboe after the double bar. The texture is now much more homophonic, with the oboe then the first violins dominating the reduced wind band and lower strings. The end of the Prelude features the intertwining "ivy and vine" of solo wind and strings above a very slow-moving chordal accompaniment embellished with harp arpeggios. The final chord returns to the wind scoring of the beginning of the Prelude, omitting all but the highest of the woodwind instruments.

Form: All of the elements so far discussed contribute to a structure which is entirely original, bearing little relationship to any of the classical forms.

Exposition (bars 1-24): Tonal centre A minor/major
Two themes, the first ending with an interrupted cadence in bars 16-17, the second overlapping it and ending with a perfect cadence in A major (bar 24).

Middle Section (bars 25-67): Shifting tonal centres
This takes the shape of a ternary structure in which the first section (bars 25-36) consists of a new melody (theme 3, labelled A in Example 68a) constructed from motives heard in the exposition plus a repeat of theme 2 (labelled B). The central episode (bars 36-44, labelled C in Example 68a) consists of an antiphonal development of motive z from theme 2. The return of the first section begins with an exact repeat of A, but B is transposed and extended so that it overlaps with:

Recapitulation 1 (bars 68-83): A minor/major modulating to E♭ minor
In bars 68-77[1] the essence of bars 2-20 returns but is severely abridged by the omission of repeats and rests and by telescoping some of the motives. The exposition is radically reharmonised and rescored. To compensate, it is

extended by further development of all of the motives leading to the climactic Tristan chord in bar 83. The first recapitulation overlaps with the second in bars 82 and 83.

Recapitulation 2 and link to coda (bars 82-94): A minor, modulations, and a return to the tonic key of A major.

All three motives return in antiphonal exchanges overlapping with:

Coda (bars 94-118): A major

Quotations from Act II and the end of the *Liebestod* lead to eventual harmonic and melodic resolution in the final plagal cadence.

Style: The intense motivic elaboration, polyphonic textures, dissonant and chromatic harmony, elusive tonality and lavish orchestration are peculiar to Wagner's mature style.

LAM 71

Bruckner: Mass in E minor (1869)

Title: Bruckner's E minor Mass was written for the dedication of a newly-built chapel in Linz cathedral. It was designed for performance in the open air, hence the scoring for double chorus and wind ensemble (the biting timbre of wind instruments is more effective outdoors than the less astringent timbre of strings).

Melody in the Sanctus: Each of the eight vocal parts is assigned a reworking of the contrapuntal motive taken from Palestrina's *Missa Brevis* (Short Mass) shown in Example 71a. It will be seen that the pitches of the first four notes of Palestrina's motive are the same as the first four notes of Bruckner's reworking of it, but that instead of a leap of a perfect 4th Bruckner leaps a major 6th. This was one of the melodic intervals which Palestrina and his contemporaries avoided (as was the 7th which Bruckner requires the second basses to sing in bar 18). The rhythm is too square and lacking in subtlety to reflect adequately the style of the renaissance master. Where Palestrina introduces a subtle syncopation (second beat of bar 3) Bruckner marches down a scale in equal crotchets. The paraphrase technique that Bruckner uses is technically similar to that which Palestrina so often used (eg LAM 3), but his melodic style lacks the gentle flow of much 16th century polyphony.

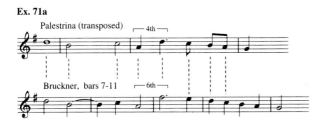

Ex. 71a

Melody in the Benedictus: There could hardly be a greater contrast between two passages in the same work than that between Bruckner's diatonic setting of the Sanctus and his chromatic setting of the Benedictus. His model in the latter was Wagner, as Examples 68a and 71b show. In the Benedictus, sequential motive y contains within it a shorter motive (x) which is itself treated sequentially in bars 6-8. This is the same as motive x in Example 68a (which Wagner also treats sequentially). It is worth noting that just as Wagner's unending melody migrates from part to part, so Bruckner's scalic countermelody in bars 6-8 of Example 71b is divided between an oboe and the first sopranos.

Ex. 71b

Harmony in the Sanctus: Bruckner's harmonic progressions are quasi-modal in their effect. In the first four bars the triads of C major, A minor, G major, E minor and A minor are entirely modal (much more so than is the case in the first four bars of LAM 3). In other passages the use of a dominant 7th chord followed by the tonic suggest the keys of G and D major (eg V^7d-Ib in G in bars 6-7 and V^7d-I in D in bars 12-13). Where Palestrina's use of dissonance is carefully controlled, Bruckner's dissonances can seem almost arbitrary (eg in bar 2, beat 2, the dotted minim C and the minim D form a 7th which is not resolved, and the same is true of the 4th from the real bass at this point (dotted minim A and minim D)).

Harmony in the Benedictus: Again the two movements are strikingly contrasted: diatonic harmony in the first, Wagnerian chromatic harmony in the second. As in Wagner it is possible to see some of the chords as self-sufficient entities, while others seem to be formed by the coincidence of chromatic contrapuntal lines. Thus the dominant 7th of C major (bars 2-3) is disguised by an accented chromatic passing-note (C♯), a chromatic lower auxiliary (A♯) and a diatonic upper auxiliary (minim C). The German 6th in A minor (last inversion) on the first beat of bar 4 resolves to chord Ic in this key, but this chord too is obscured by auxiliaries (D and B in soprano 1). Tonality becomes clearer and chords as entities become more apparent in the second system. This starts with three imperfect cadences in D minor (Ic-V, then the German 6th of D minor in last inversion resolving to V, then Ic-V again in bars 8, 9 and 10 respectively). The route back to the tonic is typical of Bruckner in chromatic mode. An A major chord (V in D minor on the last beat of bar 10) is simply juxtaposed with an F minor first inversion chord in the next bar. There can be no theoretical harmonic justification for this progression, it is simply the result of semitonal voice-leading (though retrospectively the F minor triad turns out to be a minor version of the subdominant in C major). The extract ends with two completely diatonic perfect cadences in C major.

Texture in the Sanctus: The backbone of the eight-voice polyphony is a series of four canons 2 in 1 made from Bruckner's Palestrinian motive shown in Example 71a. These are:

canon at the 5th below in alto 1, bars 1-6 (dux) and tenor 1, bars 1-7^2 (comes),

canon at the 5th below in soprano 1, bars 7-12 (dux) and bass 1, bars 7-13^2 (comes)

canon at the 4th above in bass 2, bars 13-18^3 (dux) and alto 2, bars 13-19^1 (comes)

canon at the 4th above in tenor 2, bars 20-25^1 (dux) and soprano 2, bars 20-25^3 (comes)

Around these are woven free parts in a dense contrapuntal vocal texture.

Texture in the Benedictus: Example 71b shows how the outer voices form two-part counterpoint with imitation between y and its two variants y^1 and y^2. The astringent harmony is underlined by consecutive 7ths in bars 3 and 4, and by the false relations between C♮ and C♯ (bar 3) and between D♯ and D♮ (bar 4). The contrapuntal tension and high-register woodwind and female voices (bars 1-8) contrast with the homophonic, low-register wind and male-voice texture (bars 8-9) and the a cappella homophony at the end of the extract.

Styles: Neo-renaissance in the Sanctus. Wagnerian in the Benedictus.

LAM 76

Tchaikovsky: Symphony No.5: 2nd Movement (1888)

Title: Although the title itself tells us nothing, Tchaikovsky's letters to his patron, Madame von Meck, and his inscriptions on the score bear eloquent testimony to the significance of this passionate music. Of the first movement he wrote that it represented "complete resignation before Fate, or, which is the same, before the inscrutable predestination of Providence". The fate theme which embodies the composer's resignation is heard on clarinets right at the start of the symphony (Example 76a (i)). Of particular importance is the scalic descent encompassing a 6th (x). In all of his mature works this had come to signify the malignity of fate. This motto theme appears in three of the four movements. In LAM 76 it shatters the expected return to the lyricism of the start of the movement (Example 76a (ii)).

Historical context: Tchaikovsky was above all a dramatic composer, whether writing ballet, opera or symphonic works. Nevertheless he was one of a handful of composers who successfully managed to keep the symphonic ideal alive long after its shelf life had expired (or so thought the revolutionary Wagnerians). He was influenced by minor French operatic composers such as Massenet and by indigenous Russian music. He avoided Wagnerian temptations, but was never regarded as one of the nationalist school of Russian composers (the *kuchka*, which included Borodin - LAM 74). His influence on such diverse successors as Rachmaninov (LAM 83) and Stravinsky (LAM 91) cannot be underestimated. Indeed his influence lasted well into the 20th century, not least in film music.

Above one of the lyrical melodies of this movement Tchaikovsky is said to have written "Oh, how I love you! Oh my friend!". Whether or not this is apocryphal it could well refer to the original oboe melody (Example 76b (i)) which Tchaikovsky inflates into the passionate melody of the first 12 bars of this extract (Example 76b (ii)). In another letter to Madame von Meck Tchaikovsky wrote "I have tried more than once to express in music the torment and delight of love ... I disagree with you absolutely that music cannot fully express the feelings of love. On the contrary, only music can do so." It needs no analytical skill to understand the messages the homosexual Russian composer was delivering to posterity in the two versions of this love music shown in Example 76b.

Rhythm: When the love theme (Example 76b (i)) is first heard near the beginning of the movement it is accompanied by throbbing triplet string chords which form cross-rhythms with the oboe and horn duplets. The cross-rhythms are much more urgent in LAM 76 because the accompanying wind chords are in semiquavers against the 12/8 rhythms in the strings and upper wind.

Melody: The fate theme (Example 76a) is constructed from short repeated motives circling round the notes of the tonic triad of E minor. This, together with the strong tinge of Aeolian modality, is typical of much Russian folk music. The air of resignation is further enhanced by the slow tempo and the oily timbre of the clarinet in its chalumeau register. When the fate theme returns in this extract (trombones, bar 158) it too becomes much more urgent: the tempo is now Allegro, the dynamic level *fff*, the rhythm of bars 2 and 4 is faster, motive x is compressed from two bars to one bar and it now encompasses the interval of a tritone (the infamous *diabolus in musica*).

A similar transformation is wrought upon the love theme (Example 76b). In its original form the falling contour of the first bar is repeated, in the extract it is the rising contour of the second bar that is repeated. Similarly the climax of the original melody is an appoggiatura resolving down (y) and repeated an octave lower. In the extract the highly dissonant appoggiaturas resolve upwards and are repeated ever more urgently in the rising sequence of bars 149-153 until the music reaches the most overwhelming climax of the whole movement (marked *ffff!*).

Harmony and tonality: The original fate motive (Example 76a (i)) is harmonised modally (the sharpened leading-note being heard only once). But the fate motive in LAM 76 is harmonised throughout with one chromatic diminished 7th chord. It cries out for resolution, but never achieves it since it moves, not to the expected dominant chord of D, but to another dissonance, II^7b of D minor in bars 164-165.

The original version of the love theme (Example 76b (i)) was harmonised diatonically over a tonic pedal. The theme as shown in Example 76b (ii)) is harmonised chromatically with the bass descending in contrary motion against the rising melody. In the process intense dissonances are produced, such as those shown by the double-headed arrows in Example 76b (ii). The level of dissonance increases as the climax approaches. For instance, in bars 150-151 a tenor trombone sustains an A♮ against the strings' G♯ and A♯. The climax is achieved as a French 6th in its last inversion (bar 152, beats 3-4) resolves onto VIc of D major (first beat of bar 153). The remainder of Tchaikovsky's progression is shown in Example 76c. What is particularly notable is the use of second inversion chords at the start of bars 153, 154 and 155. None of them resolve to the expected root position chords. They are contained by the contrary motion of treble and bass, but their effect is nevertheless destabilising (as the composer intended them to be). The *coup de théatre* at the sudden appearance of the fate motive is greatly enhanced by a chromatic interrupted cadence (V^7-V^{m9} of V in bars 157-158).

Ex. 76c

D major: VI_c V^7 IV_c V^7 of VI II_c II^7_c A^6 I_c V^7 I_c V^7 V^{m9} of V

Orchestral textures: The love theme in bars 146-148 is doubled at the octave above and below, then from bar 149 an extra octave is added so the theme is spread over four octaves on woodwind and strings. The contrapuntal bass line is similarly doubled in octaves by the trombones, tuba and double bass. The harmony between these polarised parts is provided by pulsating horn and trumpet chords. The texture changes with the arrival of the fate theme: this is played by trombone and bassoons accompanied by tremolo string arpeggios above the bass G♯ (tuba with tremolo double basses an octave lower plus a melodramatic drum roll).

Style and genre: Late romantic symphony.

LAM 85

Ravel: String Quartet in F major: 1st Movement (1903)

Title and context: The string quartet is a quintessentially classical genre. Ravel was only 27 when he wrote this quartet and it is dedicated "to my dear teacher, Gabriel Fauré", another reticent and classically inspired Frenchman. It follows the usual four-movement scheme of the classical quartet. The extract consists of the final bars of the first movement in which Ravel recapitulates the second subject of his sonata-form structure (bars 184-197), then, in a coda (bars 201-213) makes brief references to both the first subject (bars 201-204) and second subject again (bars 204ff).

Melody: There are two gently flowing melodies in this extract, both including repetitions of melodic fragments. The first of these themes (bars 184-190^2) has a modal hue. It starts and ends on A and its repeated motives circle around an E, a 5th above the A. Thus A becomes the tonic and E the dominant of the Phrygian mode transposed to A (ie A, B♭, C, D, E, F, G, A). These two notes are emphasised in the link to the modified repeat of the first melody (viola, bars 192-196^3). But this repeat inflects the former dominant (E♮) to an E♭, and, since there are only five pitches (B♭, C, D, E♭ and F) the tonality of the melody becomes cloudy. In the remainder of this section (bars 196-200) the triplet figure becomes a mesmeric viola ostinato which links the first theme of the extract to the second (it continues under the first violin melody in bars 201-203, but the E♭ becomes a D♯, the 6th degree of the scale of F♯ major, the key of the second melody).

The second melody (bars 201-213) begins pentatonically (C♯, D♯ E♯, G♯, A♯ in violin 1, bars 201-206^1) and ends pentatonically (F, G, A, B♭, C in violin 1 bars 209-213). Neither of these scales of themselves conclusively establishes a key, but, although the tonic note of F♯ major is absent from the first and the leading-note of F major is absent from the second, the harmony clarifies these two tonal centres.

Harmony and tonality: Modal and pentatonic melodies are harmonised with a variety of dissonant and sometimes non-funtional chords, often in parallel motion , but locked into tonal centres by cello fifths (whether melodic leaps or harmonic intervals) and harmonic filling between these outer parts. Thus there can be no doubt about the F major tonality of bars 184-197 despite the modal E♭s (suggesting the Mixolydian mode: F, G, A, B♭, C, D, E♭, F). The tonic chord of F major in bars 184-187 is defined by the second viola and cello, but a major 7th is added by the first violin and viola. This major 7th chord moves down a step to the flattened leading-note in bar 188, and the cadence is formed by the dominant major 9th of the dominant (bar 190) and a dominant 13th (bar 191) resolving back to the tonic (bar 192). But this time the tonic chord is coloured, not by a diatonic 7th (E♮), but by a flattened 7th (E♭) which sounds throughout bars 192-203 (changing enharmonically to a D♯).

It is in this section that tonality begins to melt as Ravel gradually introduces more and more chromatic notes, notably in the whole-tone cluster in the first three beats of bar 198 (B, C♯, D♯/E♭, F and G). A pedal (cello, bars 198-203) becomes specifically dominant in function in bars 201-203 where it supports the dominant 13th of F♯ major: root C♯, 3rd E♯, 7th B♮, major 9th D♯ (enharmonically notated as E♭), and 13th A♯. When this resolves to chord IV in bar 204 it forms an interrupted cadence similar to those in the coda of the *Concert Prelude to Tristan and Isolde* (LAM 68, bars 94-95 et seq). From the B major chord of bars 204-206 (note that all three semibreves in these bars should have natural signs before them, not sharps as printed in some editions of the *Anthology*) consecutive root position major triads move down a whole tone scale to an E♭ major chord on the flattened leading-note of F major. Twice a modal cadence consisting of ♭VII and I is heard (bars 209-210 and 210-211), but the movement ends with a most unusual major 9th chord on the supertonic resolving to the tonic itself.

Texture: The French delight in subtle variations of instrumental colour is apparent throughout the extract:

In bars 184-191 the melody is allotted to the first violin doubled at the

15th below by the viola. This is supported by the second violin's harmonic filling and the cello's pizzicato fifths.

In bars 192-197 the viola melody is heard against a violin countermelody with the second violin and cello continuing their accompanimental roles.

In bars 198-203 a sustained minor 7th (second violin and cello) supports the first violin melody and the viola ostinato.

In bars 204-210 the texture thickens to five parts (cello double-stopped 5ths) then six parts (violin double-stopped octaves). In the last two bars the violins sustain bowed chords while the cello and viola play a pizzicato arpeggio and two tonic chords.

Form: Recapitulation of the second subject together with the coda form a sonata-form movement.

Style: Neoclassical in formal structure and modality, impressionist in harmony and texture.

LAM 86

Mahler: Ruckert Lieder: Um Mitternacht (1905)

Title: Ruckert (1788-1866) was a German lyric poet whose *Kindertotenlieder* (Children's Death Songs) were set as a song cycle by Mahler (both composers suffered the deaths of their children). *Lieder* = songs. Mahler set five of Ruckert's poems in 1901-2, but they were not performed until a few years later, possibly in 1905. Each of these lyrics evokes a moment in time and freezes it, as though to preserve it from decay. In *Um Mitternacht* the moment is midnight. The poet looks at the myriad stars and thinks of the endless darkness of space. No vision of light comforts him, [he is alone like all souls, and cannot by his own strength gain victory over the indifference of creation. Defeated, he resigns himself to the Lord of death and life who keeps watch at midnight.] (The passage of my paraphrase of Ruckert's poem in square brackets is not represented in LAM 86).

Melody and motive: The first 22 bars consist almost entirely of manipulations of the first three motives shown in Example 86.

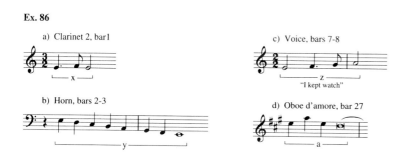

Ex. 86

a) Clarinet 2, bar 1

b) Horn, bars 2-3

c) Voice, bars 7-8
"I kept watch"

d) Oboe d'amore, bar 27

Motive x occurs every time Ruckert's refrain *Um Mitternacht* is repeated (usually with the first clarinet part above it, though it is heard on its own as early as the flute entry in the second bar). This motive is based on the dominant of the home key (A minor/major), and this degree of the scale is even more pronounced in the first vocal entry (where the E♮ lasts for six long minim beats). Motive y (Example 86b) is first heard as a complete Phrygian scale (partially repeated by flutes in bars 4-6, by a bassoon and contrabassoon in bars 6-7, and by the voice in bars 11-12). By bar 8 the tonic, A minor, has been established, so when motive y is transposed down a 5th in bars 12-13 (bassoon) it is heard as a descending melodic minor scale starting and ending on the tonic. In bar 18 the motive becomes semitonal with the addition of the sharpened leading-note (the only time this key-defining note is heard in the first 22 bars, and even then it falls to the flattened 7th instead of rising to the tonic). The bassoon and contrabassoon part in bars 19-20 is a repeat of the same version of motive y as was heard in bars 6-7, but it is now welded to motive x. In the final appearance of this motive (voice, bars 32³-34³) the descent from the upper to the lower dominant becomes chromatic and again ends with motive x superimposed on its final note.

Motive z (Example 86c) rises by step from the dominant to the tonic and is then repeated with a different rhythm (*und aufgeblickt*) to reach the highest note in the first section (perhaps suggesting the raising of the head to contemplate the heavens). In bar 13 an exact repeat of this phrase begins, but it sinks back to the dominant with the words *Um Mitternacht*. The motive is heard again in bars 21-23 (where it links the two sections) and bars 30-31 (where it is in the tonic major).

The melodies in the second section are longer ("I sent my thoughts to the far bounds of dark space"). The first of them begins with a rising perfect 4th (bar 23) followed by a rising perfect 5th (bar 24). These intervals are taken up in a very long chromatic melody played on an oboe d'amore (bars 27-33). This time it is part of a new motive (a in Example 86d, which begins with a rising perfect 4th like that in bar 23) which is repeated in modified form in the next bar. The leap of a perfect 5th returns in bar 29 but the descent now winds chromatically all the way from this top G♯ down to the B♭ in bar 33 (a note which sounds like the flattened supertonic of A major/minor, but which never resolves to the tonic). The rising perfect 4th appears again on the word "light" (*Licht*, bar 31), but instead of being followed by the perfect 5th the voice falls in the version of motive y which we have already discussed.

Harmony and tonality: In the first section (bars 1-22) the harmony is entirely based on the notes of the Aeolian mode (A, B, C, D, E, F, G, A), and the chords are limited to consonant triads of A minor, D minor (the B♮ in bar 15 sounds like an appoggiatura above a D minor chord), and E minor. The only strong dissonance is the appoggiatura played by the oboe d'amore in bar 17 (which resolves to the 3rd of a D minor triad in second inversion). It is notable that this dissonance emphasises the modality of the first section (G♮ is the flattened 7th degree of A minor). The tonal centre of this section is A minor, but the avoidance of the sharpened leading note (apart from bar 18 where the G♯ sounds like a chromatic passing-note rather than a degree of the scale) and functional harmony casts a modal hue over the whole section. In addition, the emphasis on the dominant, particularly in the bass, destabilises the tonality so that the music sounds like a question (what is the meaning of the starry heavens?).

For most of the second section, the key (A major) is much clearer despite the chromaticism. This is because the tonic chord is now used in association with "real" dominant chords. For instance the progression in bars 23-27 is clearly heading for the inverted perfect cadence in A major:

I/V^{7}c of V, II^{7}b/Ib, V^7 of V/V^7/Ib

This progression is, however, overlaid with decorations which are here identified by vocal syllables:

ich: appoggiatura
dacht and *aus*: suspensions
dunk: accented passing-note (G♯)
Schran: double appoggiatura (A♯ and F♯).

At its most chromatic, however, the tonality is almost submerged by a welter of decorations. In bar 33 the underlying progression is I, IVb and the Neapolitan 6th chord of A major/minor, but there is a double appoggiatura above chord I (beat 1), an accented passing-note (B♮) and a chromatic passing-note (C♮) above IVb, and a chromatic accented passing-note above the Neapolitan 6th. The vocal dissonances and their resolutions form a whole-tone scale (like a chromatic scale this scale is atonal) and the Neapolitan 6th completely fails to resolve as the voice returns to the dominant of A minor.

Texture: The texture consists of a polyphonic web of motives and independent melodic lines in which the voice is most often one of the contrapuntal strands. For instance in bars 4-6 the voice sings a freely augmented version of motive x against motive y on the flute. Both are imitated (by clarinet and bassoon respectively). In bars 7-8 the voice and horn are doubled (motive z), but in the next two bars the voice goes its own way. The spare soloistic counterpoint of the first section gives way to more luxuriant counterpoint reaching maximum density when a complete chromatic scale from upper to lower tonic in the bass (another version of y in bars 27-31) supports the chromatic extension of motive a (oboe d'amore) and motive x (voice) together with free wind parts. The song is remarkable in its chamber-like scoring for solo wind, with drums, harp and piano entering at the climax in the last verse (not shown in LAM 86).

Form: By the use of recurring motives Mahler mirrors the verse-form of the poem, every stanza of which begins and ends with the words *Um Mitternacht*. In the extract the first verse (bars 1-22) is set in A minor, the second in the tonic major.

Style and genre: Late romantic orchestral Lied.

LAM 91

Stravinsky: The Rite of Spring, Part I: Auguries of Spring (1913)

Title: "One day [in 1910 in St. Petersburg] I had a fleeting vision which came to me as a complete surprise ... I saw in my imagination a solemn pagan rite – sage, elders, seated in a circle, watching a young girl dance herself to death. They were sacrificing her to propitiate the god of spring. Such was the theme of *Le Sacre du printemps*." (Stravinsky)

This was the vision from which the ballet score emerged three years later. It was subtitled "Scenes from Pagan Russia". Both the title and subtitle are explicit: this is not a "story ballet" in the classical tradition, rather is it a series of tableaux depicting an imagined ritual sacrifice. The extract is taken from the beginning of the first of these scenes in which adolescents and the sacrificial victim invoke the god of spring. Written in 1911, it was the first and most infamous part of the ballet which Stravinsky composed.

Rhythm: Although written in 2/4 time, the stamping chords of the first eight bars are not metrical (every string chord receives exactly the same down-bow accentuation as the next until the accent marks appear). If a classically-programmed listener were to imply duple time his expectations would be defeated by the savage sforzando horn chords which sound at random intervals of 2, 6, 3, 4 and 5-quaver intervals. Duple time is asserted by the ostinati in bars 84-87, but this metrical pattern lasts only four bars before the stamping chords and irregularly-spaced wind chords return.

Once duple metre has been firmly established (as in bars 98-100) syncopation against the beat is a possibility (as in the off-beat brass chords in bars 101, 103 and 104). In these bars the violas are in cross-rhythm with the rest of the orchestra (ie triplets against duplets).

One feature of Russian folk melody is the repetition of short motives with rhythmic displacement. Example 91a shows a melody which Stravinsky noted in his sketchbook for The Rite. It will be seen that the three-note figure of two semiquavers and a quaver (x) is first heard starting on the third quaver of the bar, then it is displaced to start on the second quaver before returning to its original position. A similar process can be seen in Example 91b where a descending semitonal figure of five notes contains a triplet and a duplet rhythm. In (i) (trumpet, bars 93-94) the triplet is on the first beat of the bar, in (ii) (oboes, bar 95) it has been displaced to the second beat of the bar, and in (iii) (first violins, bars 96-97) the semitonal descent is extended downwards by using triplets on both beats of the bar.

Melody: Apart from this semitonal figure the only other theme is a Russian folk melody which winds conjunctly round on itself as a short motive repeats (y in Example 91c (i)). This melody is not heard in its original form. Instead Stravinsky displaces every other note to produce the ostinato figure in the first violins starting at bar 105 (Example 91c (ii)). In the flute part, in the same passage the original scalic melody is heard on every quaver, but it is decorated with octave leaps (8ve) and upper auxiliary notes (a), the whole being doubled two octaves above by the piccolos.

Rite caused a full scale riot at its first performance). Here we have space to consider just one aspect or the two composers' styles, that of harmony. They both used chords which are now known by the titles of the works in which they occur: the "Tristan Chord" and the "Rite Chord". These are both dissonances, but otherwise they are totally different from each other. Where the Tristan Chord resolves to the relative consonance of a dominant 7th and initiates a whole series of tonal climaxes, the Rite Chord repudiates conventional tonality: instead of resolving it is simply repeated (280 times!) without any resolution at all. All late 19th century and early 20th century composers had to respond to Wagner's extremely dissonant and chromatic harmony (which yet remained tonal). Schoenberg chose to take Wagner's developmental path to its logical conclusion in his expressionist works (eg LAM 89 and 90). Stravinsky decided to ignore the challenge altogether and forge new styles based on completely different premises.

Harmony and tonality: Stravinsky's chords are most often derived from the triads and 7th chords of earlier periods, but they are emptied of their functional behaviour in relation to a specific key. Instead they are chosen for their colouristic effect or sonority in relation to the particular ritual being enacted by the dancers. In the extract, vibrant, dissonant chords are aggregates of two or more simple chords. This bitonality is evident in the famous "Rite Chord" heard in the strings in the first eight bars. It consists of a triad of F♭ major (alias E major) in root position played by cellos and double basses (remember that the basses sound an

octave below printed pitch) plus an E♭ seventh chord in first inversion played by violins and violas (some refer to this chord as a dominant 7th, but this is confusing since it never functions as a dominant chord). In bars 84-87 the top three notes of this 7th chord (B♭, D♭ and E♭) be come an ostinato played on the cor anglais (remember that this instrument sounds a perfect 5th below printed pitch). Similarly the F♭ major chord becomes an arpeggio of E major (cellos, bars 84 and 86). To these two broken chords, the bassoons add C major and E minor arpeggios thus adding more chords to the bitonal "Rite Chord": the music is now polytonal.

Another method of achieving dissonant but sonorous chords is to pile 4ths or 5ths on top of each other (instead of the 3rds used in traditional harmony). A chord consisting of superimposed perfect 5ths can be heard in the brass parts in bars 101-104: reading upwards the constituent notes are E♭ (horn), B♭, F, C, G (trumpets in C) and D (trumpet in D). Similarly the chord at the end of bar 109 consists of piled-up perfect 4ths (D, G, C, F, B♭, E♭ reading upwards from the lowest note in the second violin part).

Texture:
a) Bars 76-83: Repeated 8-part string chords doubled by detached 8-part horn chords.
b) Bars 84-87: Combination of three melodic ostinati.
c) Bars 88-97: As bars 76-83 but with the cor anglais ostinato, new syncopated detached wind chords and the triplet motive superimposed over the Rite Chord.
d) Bars 98-109: Polytonal ostinati (cor anglais, violas, cellos and basses) with bassoon and oboe pedal form a background for syncopated brass chords and heterophonic flute and piccolo parts (see Examples 91c (ii) and (iii).

Unlike romantic scoring these sections do not overlap: each of them ends abruptly and is immediately replaced with the next texture.

Instrumentation and orchestration: The Rite requires one of the largest orchestras ever assembled. In addition to the conventional string band Stravinsky demands 18 woodwind, 18 brass and a percussion section to match. Unlike most romantic composers (eg Wagner – LAM 68) Stravinsky's orchestration highlights the uncontaminated timbre of each instrument or section by avoiding doubling for the most part. Although the horns play the same notes as the strings in the first eight bars their tone colour can be clearly distinguished from the strings because they only play detached chords. In bars 84-87 the timbre of each solo instrument can be clearly distinguished, as can the solo muted trumpet in bar 94, the oboes in octaves in bar 95, and the first violins in bar 96 (clearly distinguished from the lower strings by playing pizzicato). The cor anglais ostinato is never doubled by any other instrument. When there is a brief spell of doubling this is usually confined to one section (as is the case with the bassoon and oboe pedal in bars 102-109 and the flute section in the same bars).

LAM 97

Bartók: Mikrokosmos, Volume IV: From the Island of Bali (1926)

Title: Mikrokosmos means little world: the little world in this case being six volumes of teaching pieces, beginning with five finger exercises, and ending with a set of six difficult Dances in Bulgarian Rhythms. It is a little world in two other senses. Firstly Bartók explores a huge range of compositional techniques and styles, each short piece demonstrating one or more of them. Secondly Bartók combines Western compositional techniques with melodies derived from Eastern European folk sources. In this case he casts his net even wider to evoke the atmosphere and the particular scale-forms of Indonesian gamelan music. There is no evidence that the two notations of Balinese gamelan music shown on page 360 represent music which Bartók actually heard in recorded form (the present author found them whilst searching for gamelan music which used scales similar to those upon which *From the Island of Bali* is based). Indeed, despite Kuta village being a popular holiday resort, it is highly unlikely that the composer did hear the precise ostinato motif shown in LAM 97a. What is more likely is that Bartók heard gamelan music using similar tunings to those in a) and/or b), perhaps on the radio (his ear was so keen that it would have taken only one playing for him to register and remember the relative pitches of whatever gamelan music he came across).

Rhythm and melody in LAM 97a: The larger the gong or metallophone the slower the rhythm. Thus the gongs numbered 11 and 12 alternate every bar (see the *Appendix* to the *Anthology* for the names of the instruments represented by numbers to the left of the score). Gongs 9 and 10 play twice or four times as fast. The ostinato motif itself is played in crotchets and quavers of metallophones 8 and 7 respectively while metallophones 1-4 provide complex syncopated rhythms with the semiquaver as the basic unit of time. All of these instruments play between one or more notes of the same pentatonic scale (D, E♭, F, A and B♭).

Melody in LAM 97b: Like the ostinato played by the metallophones on the seventh stave of 97a, this melody is pentatonic, but the baro tuning consists of the notes D♯, E, F, A♯ and B.

Melody in LAM 97c: Like the melodies of both 97a and 97b the melody in the first section (bars 12-16²) is pentatonic (B, C, F, G♭ and A♭♭). Like metallophones 1 + 3 and 2 + 4, Bartók's melody is doubled, the former at the octave, the latter at the 15th. Example 97a shows how the same motives appear in both 97b and 97c (F♮ to A♯ = F♮ to B♭ enharmonically notated: both in acoustic terms are perfect 4ths). Both consist of a rising semitone, perfect 4th and another semitone (x) and both are inverted (xI, which because of the symmetry of the motive is also a retrograde).

Ex. 97a   Motives common to the Pengawak
and "From the Island of Bali"

(i) Pengawak bar 1

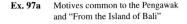

(ii) Bartók bars 12-13 and 15-16

Example 97b shows that the altered motive (y) in the last section of the Bartók (bars 23-30) is almost identical with the end of the melodic line played by metallophones 7 in the ostinato motive. Again both are inverted (yI).

Historical context: As a student at the Budapest Conservatoire Bartók was awoken from compulsory and stupefying academic exercises in sub-Brahmsian style by a performance of *Also sprach Zarathustra* (LAM 80). Inspired by this he produced a number of Straussian works including a gigantic tone poem in seven movements called *Kossuth* (a Hungarian national hero). But other influences soon began to contribute towards his unique idiom. Bach's contrapuntal fireworks are evident even in the little piano piece from which our extract has been taken. His profound understanding of Eastern European folk music (developed by research in the field with his compatriot, Zoltán Kodály) is evident in his own music as early as his *First String Quartet* (LAM 87). Debussy influenced his more impressionist works (especially the "night music" in the slow movements of his instrumental works).

He was above all a composer who breathed fresh life into Beethovenian forms and genres, as his set of six string quartets demonstrate. But this was not coldly calculated neoclassicism à la Stravinsky, for he balanced abstract forms and intellectual conceits with a passionate expressiveness and sincerity which is rare in 20th century music. In the closing years of his life he was able to return to unashamedly tonal music and communicate directly with ordinary men and women in such standard items of the modern concert repertoire as his *Third Piano Concerto* and the *Concerto for Orchestra*. This he did without compromising his artistic ideals (though the cultural

Ex. 97b Motives common to the Ostinato and "From the Island of Bali"

(i) Bartók bars 23-24¹ and 25¹⁻²

(ii) Ostinato, stave 7

Rhythm in LAM 97c: In the left hand part of bars 21-22, Bartók omits the first note of motive xI (see Example 97c (ii)). This reduces the motive to a three-note figure which he immediately repeats three times. The result (clearly shown by the slurs) is a cross-rhythm against the established 4/4 metre (only the second of the four groups of three quavers in this ostinato begins on a strong beat, the others begin off the beat or on a weak beat). In the same bars Bartók constructs another ostinato from motive x (repeated twice in the left hand part). This too runs counter to the metre because the motive always starts off the beat and is cross-phrased to the next strong beat. These two parts form a more complex cross-rhythm with each other which is similar to phrasing in some later 20th century minimalist music (one more repetition of the two motives would bring the two parts back to the beginning of the cycle).

Ex. 97c Canons and octatonic collection used by Bartók in bars 16³-22

(i) Canon at the 6th below

(ii) Canon by inversion

(iii) Octatonic scale derived from x and xI

Textures in LAM 97c: The first and last sections are monophonic (melody doubled at the octave or 15th). At the start of the middle section the melody of bars 12-14² is heard transposed to start on G♯ (right hand, bars 16³-18²). This is imitated by the left hand to form a strict canon at the 6th below (see Example 97c (i)). In bars 18³-21¹ the right hand melody is inverted but the left hand part is repeated exactly as it was in the first canon. This produces a canon by inversion. The rest of this section is in free two-part counterpoint.

Harmony in LAM 97c: Example 97c shows that a specifically Western scale of the 20th century can be derived from the collection of 12 pitches in bars 16³-22. This octatonic scale consists of alternating semitones and tones (seven of the eight pitches of an octatonic scale can be clearly heard in the upper wind and soprano parts at the start of LAM 99). When the number of available pitches is limited in this way it imparts a particular flavour to the harmony (compare the extremes of music based entirely on the black notes of the piano with the systematic use of all 12 chromatic degrees in the music of Webern: the former sounds relatively consonant, the latter extremely dissonant). In this piece the two-note chords articulated on the beat are all consonant apart from the 9th and 2nd in bar 22. Some of the chords may look peculiar because of the way the two pitches are notated, but they sound like the consonant enharmonic equivalent (eg the middle C and the G♯ above it on the second beat of bar 19 is in effect a minor 6th - C and A♭).

LAM 102

Walton: Belshazzar's Feast (1931)

Title and context: The extract is taken from an oratorio based on texts from the Old Testament Book of Daniel, from the Book of Psalms, and from the Revelation of St John the Divine. The libretto begins with a prophetic judgement upon the unfaithful Jewish race: *Thus spake Isiah: Thy sons that thou shalt beget shall be taken away and be eunuchs in the palace of the King of Babylon.* The prophesy is fulfilled: the Jews are taken into captivity by Belshazzar the King who summons a thousand of his lords to a magnificent orgiastic feast. Running through the savage choral rejoicing is a violent syncopated orchestral motive (Example 102a). The height of blasphemy is reached when the King orders his lords to join him in praising the heathen gods of gold, silver, iron, wood, stone and brass by drinking from the golden vessels which his father, Nebuchadnezzar, had taken from the Jews' temple in Jerusalem. The climax of the feast comes when the King's princes, wives and concubines pledge his health, crying out *Thou, O King, art King of Kings: O King, live for ever!*

It is at this point that *there came forth fingers of a man's hand* writing *Thou art weighed in the balance and found wanting* (LAM 102). This is the second divine judgement. The first led to the captivity of the Jews, this one leads to the death of Belshazzar, the fall of the Babylonian Empire, and the freedom of the Jews. Examples 102a and b show how Walton links the two events by preceding the sung text with the same trombone fanfare, by using the same forces (a cappella male voices), the same type of rhythm (both are determined by the rhythms of spoken English), and the same vicious dissonance (a minor triad surmounted by

Historical context: English choral music in the inter-war years (the 1920's and 1930's) was still dominated by 19th century oratorios such as Mendelssohn's *Elijah* (LAM 64). Elgar had breathed new life into our venerable tradition, but his choral masterpiece, *The Dream of Gerontius* (LAM 81) hardly expanded style and technique beyond the frontiers of tonality which Wagner had explored half a century earlier (in operas such as *Tristan and Isolde* – LAM 68). Through the patronage of the Sitwell family Walton had become a true European, familiar with the ground-breaking work of Stravinsky (LAM 91) and Schoenberg (LAM 89 and 90). From the former he learned about rhythmic complexity, dissonant harmony and brilliant orchestral colour. From the latter he took note of the dramatic possibilities of atonality, though he never espoused the sort of serial technique which Schoenberg and his disciples Webern (LAM 100) and Berg (LAM 103) pursued.

By the time he began work on *Belshazzar's Feast* Walton had already mastered the Stravinskian "cross-over" styles of jazz-cum-high-art in his parodistic entertainment *Façade* (LAM 96). All of these elements are apparent even in the narrow confines of our extract from *Belshazzar's Feast*: Schoenbergian atonality serves him well in the sinister "judgement music" of pages 370-371 (the word *slain* even takes the crossed stems used by Schoenberg in his *Sprechstimme* - LAM 90), while Stravinskian rhythmic complexity and quasi-jazz rhythms pervade the Jewish celebrations of pages 372-373. But perhaps the most important

Ex. 102

a) Belshazzar's Feast, bars 0-4

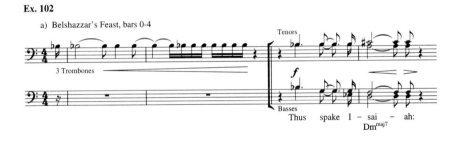

b) Bars 9-10 of LAM 102

a major 7th from the root: D minor plus C♯ in Example 102a, and F♯ minor plus E♯ in Example 102b).

It is now the turn of the Jews to rejoice, but not before Walton makes another connection. In the orchestral introduction (LAM page 372) to Psalm 81 (page 373) the violent syncopated orchestral motive in G minor (Example 102c) is transformed into an orchestral motive in F major (x in Example 102d). The rest of

c) Motive from the Babylonian feast music

d) Bars 30-35 of LAM 102

the oratorio is a complete reversal of the first part. The lamentations of the Jews is replaced with the lamentations of the Babylonians, and the heathen worship of idols is replaced with the praises of the God of Jacob. Thus our extract comes at the dramatic turning point of this biblical epic.

Rhythm:
Bars 2, 13 and 15: Recitative in which the soloist replicates the free rhythms of speech and is at liberty to bend the notated rhythms in the melismas.
Bars 3-8: Recitative in which the percussion parts in 4/4 time dictate a precise observance of Walton's notated recitative (which itself imitates the rhythm of declaimed English).
Bars 10-11: As bars 3-8, but the controlling factor here is the necessity of achieving precise ensemble from a large group of singers.
Bars 20-47: Highly syncopated counterpoint. Example 102d shows one of Walton's rhythmic techniques. Having set up an underlying triple metre, the composer maintains this in the bass part of bars 32-36 (the bass changes with each crotchet beat). In the uppermost part motive y is extracted from motive x and this three-note motive is repeated to form dotted-crotchet beats (ie, the melody is in 6/8 time). The two parts thus form a hemiolaic cross-rhythm.

Melody and tonality: The near-atonal chromaticism of the judgement (pages 370-371) contrasts strongly with the clear F major diatonicism of the Jews' rejoicing (pages 372-373). The use of a ritualistic monotone in bar 4 and bars 6-7 is hardly melodic, but no less effective for that.

Harmony: The chords on page 370 are in the nature of sound effects (and the left hand part of the piano reduction is an approximation to the untuned Hammer-House-of-Horror percussion effects). The return of the "judgmental" minor-triad-plus-major-7th in bars 10-11 has already been noted, but another highly dissonant effect in these bars is the false relation between the E♯ in the first tenors (*and found*) and the E♮ in the second tenors (*want*). Even more strident is the simultaneous false relation between the second tenor E♮ and the bass E♯ (indicated by the curved line and the letters "fr" above the stave in Example 102b). The vocal *chord* in bar 14 is shouted so that the pitches are (to say the least) inexact. The harmony on pages 372-373, though dissonant, is functional and largely diatonic: most of the chromaticisms are passing dissonances, eg the chords on the first beats of bars 33-35 in Example 102d are all inversions of the tonic chord of F major.

Texture: Four distinct types of texture are used to highlight the text:
a) bars 2, 13 and 15: unaccompanied recitative (monophony),
b) bars 3-8: accompanied recitative (a 20th century reinterpretation of 17th century monody such as LAM 8),
c) bars 10-11: choral homophony,
d) bars 20-47: largely two-part counterpoint with orchestral harmonic filling (in bars 42³-45 the sopranos and tenors in octaves form two-part counterpoint with the octaves sung by the altos and basses, but this texture is increased to three-part counterpoint by the independent orchestral bass).

LAM 103

Berg: Violin Concerto: Coda (1935)

Title and context: On 6th April 1914 Berg attended a concert in Vienna at which five cantatas by Bach were performed. Berg wrote enthusiastically to Schoenberg saying what a powerful impression the music had made on him. One of the five cantatas was *O Ewigkeit, du Donnerwort* (O Eternity, thou awesome word). There are two cantatas by Bach with this title. The one Berg heard (BWV 60) is a dialogue between Fear (of death) and Hope (of eternal life).

Twenty-one years later Berg was commissioned to write a violin concerto. As he was about to begin work on it he heard of the death of eighteen-year old Manon Gropius, the daughter of Mahler's widow by her second marriage. Berg and Manon were mutually affectionate, and it is to her that the concerto is dedicated ("To the memory of an angel"). This tragedy and Berg's recollection of the remarkable chorale from Bach's *Cantata No. 60* helped determine the unusual form of the concerto and its programmatic content.

It falls into two movements, the first containing a portrait of Manon as a beautiful, lively young woman. The second begins with an Allegro, most of which is an extended accompanied cadenza in which the soloist and orchestra seem to alternate between fear and hope (as in Bach's dialogue). Eventually the music builds to a catastrophic climax in which the composer directly confronts death (marked *Hohepunkt des "Allegros"* in the score). After this the music gradually subsides and leads, without pause, into an Adagio which begins with the chorale melody, *Es ist genung*, from Cantata No. 60. This is played on the violin an octave lower than the melody of LAM 103b, but is otherwise identical to it. In the original chorale, bars 1-6 then 15-17 are repeated. In the concerto these repeats are played with Bach's original harmonies by four clarinets (sounding remarkably like an organ stop). In the score, the text of the complete chorale is printed beneath the violin part and above the clarinets' repeats. The dialogue (in both the cantata and the concerto) is now over: the words are of resignation and hope - "It is enough ... my Jesus comes, goodnight O World, I go to heavenly rest." The rest of the Adagio consists of two variations on the chorale, references to the first movement, and the coda (LAM 103c).

Thus, although simply entitled "Concerto", the work is also a programmatic requiem for Manon.

Historical and formal context: The coda is a summation of the most important thematic material of the second movement of the concerto. The concerto itself partakes of many of the essential features of that typically romantic genre, the tone poem (see LAM 65 and 80). In the coda Berg reconciles the chorale melody with his own tone row in such a way that they literally reflect each other and end on the same note (G, the tonic of the second most important tonal centre of the whole concerto). Similarly the perfect fifths of the first two bars of the concerto are reversed so that, in the last two bars, the bass reaches down to a B♭, the tonic of the most important tonal centre of the entire concerto. The final cadences are formed with chords derived from the last six notes of the row. All of this would signify little if it were not for the fact that Berg has chosen his materials with such care that the coda is more than a simple valediction. After hearing the whole work it seems to embody in music the words of Berg's contemporary, TS Eliot "In my beginning is my end. In my end is my beginning" (*Four Quartets, East Coker*).

Berg wrote only five serial compositions, and even in these he bends the Schoenbergian rules to achieve an extremely chromatic yet often tonal style which has more to do with romanticism than with the clinical modernism of composers such as Webern (eg LAM 100). His style has as much to do with Mahler (whom both he and his teacher, Schoenberg, regarded very highly). It cannot be a coincidence that the concerto ends with the same chord as Mahler's equally valedictory hybrid symphony-cum-song cycle, *Das Lied von der Erde*. The last movement, "The farewell" repeats the word *Ewig* (for ever ...) over an equally memorable chord of the added 6th, which, like Berg's final chord, gradually disappears into silence.

Ex. 103a

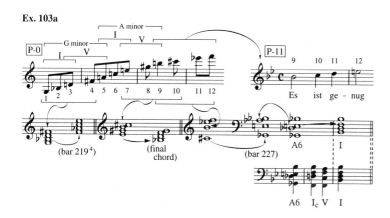

Ex. 103b

Ex. 103c

(i) First two bars of the concerto

P-3   P-0

1 3 5 7 7 5 3 1   1 3 5 7 7 5 3 1

(ii) Last two bars of the concerto

P-0

1 3 5 7 7 5 3 1

wie aus der Ferne

P-3 ⟶ 7 5 3 1 1

Melody: In the coda, the chorale melody (LAM 103b) is juxtaposed with the dodecaphonic row or series upon which the whole concerto is based (LAM 103a). The chorale melody divides into six phrases, each ending with a pause mark. The whole melody is heard in the coda: phrases 1-3 are played by two flutes in bars 214-219, phrase 4 is played by an oboe in bars 219-222, and phrase 5 (Molto adagio) by the soloist in bars 222^4-223^3. Phrase 6 (melodically a repeat of phrase 5) is played in augmentation by the first trumpet in bars 223^4-225^2 and then echoed an octave lower by two horns (bars 225^3-228^3).

A tone row is, by its very nature, chromatic. The chorale melody (apart from two notes) is entirely diatonic (in the key of B♭ major). One of the reasons Berg chose to order the 12 chromatic tones as he did is that the triads suggest diatonic keys (G minor and A minor as shown in Example 103a), while the final four notes form a segment of a whole-tone scale which corresponds with phrase 1 of the chorale melody (as shown on the upper stave of Example 103a where P-0 is the untransposed prime order, and P-11 the prime order transposed up eleven semitones). In this way the conflicting styles of the two melodic elements of the coda are partially reconciled.

This is evident at the start of the extract where the first phrase of the chorale melody (flutes, bars 214-215) is imitated by the soloist whose whole-tone segment is serially extended by manipulations of retrograde inversions of the row (Example 103b).

As phrases 5/6 of the chorale melody descend towards the goal of the final tonic note (B♭) in bars 222^4-228, so prime orders of the row in solo strings mount towards the subsidiary tonic of the concerto (G minor). This process begins with P-7 on a double bass (bars 222^4-223^2), continues with P-6 on a cello (bars 223^3-224^3), P-5 on a viola, a truncated form of P10 played by the leader (the first and 10th notes of the row are omitted), and P-2 starting on the soloist's A♮ in bar 226 and ending on the sustained G♮ in the last three bars of the concerto. Underneath this G♮ stopped horns play C♯, B♮, A♮ and G♮. This descending whole-tone segment is an inversion of the soloist's last four notes which were, of course, the same as the first four notes of the chorale melody. Since the four notes span a tritone (exactly bisecting an octave), both prime order and inversion start and end on the same notes (C♯ and G♮ respectively). This conclusively cements the relationship between the chorale and Berg's tone row.

There remains one last relationship to bind the whole concerto together. In the first two bars of the first movement Berg manipulates his as-yet-unheard row by omitting the even numbered notes and reversing the result when he reaches note 7. This produces the pyramids of perfect 5ths which can be seen in Example 103c (i), the first pyramid starting on the tonic note of B♭, the second, played on the open strings of the solo violin, starting on the subsidiary tonic note of G♮. Example 103c (ii) shows how Berg reverses the order of these two pyramids as the strings *wie aus der Ferne* (as though from afar), wind their way down to the primary tonic note of B♭.

Harmony and tonality: It is obvious that the first nine notes of Berg's prime order form interlocking triads which could be verticalised as chords suggestive of tonal centres (as Example 103a shows). Indeed Berg uses every possible collection of notes from his row to form serial harmonies such as those in the wind parts which accompany the first three phrases of the chorale melody on page 374 of the *Anthology*. One example of a dissonant chord formed by verticalisation of the first four notes of the prime order is shown in Example 103a, a minor triad surmounted by the note a major 7th above the root. If this chord is transposed up a minor 7th (shown by the first arrow below the second stave of Example 103a) it will be seen that it contains the same notes as the chord on the last beat of bar 219. Similarly the next chord is formed from notes 3-6 of the prime order. The harmony on these two pages is atonal (though the presence of the diatonic chorale melody does hint at the tonal centre that is to be firmly established in the last bars of the concerto).

By verticalisations of carefully chosen segments of the row, Berg assembles chords which, though chromatic, clearly function within a specific key. This is the case with the last two chords of the concerto. Example 103a shows that a verticalisation of notes 7-10 of the row forms a chord of the added 6th (a major triad on E with a major 6th above the root). If this chord is transposed down an augmented 4th (shown by the second arrow below the second stave in Example 103a) the result is identical with the chord of the added 6th in the last two bars of the concerto.

The next chord in Example 103a is a verticalisation of notes 9-12 of the row. If this is transposed in a similar fashion to the previous chords (shown by another arrow) the result will be identical with the chord in bar 227 (the F♯ in the tuba part has been enharmonically notated in Example 103a). It will be seen that this chord is an Italian 6th in B♭ major (ie the flattened submediant, G♭, plus a major 3rd above it, B♭, and an augmented 6th above the root, E♮). The A♭ is a stranger, but it does not alter the function of the chord, as a simple experiment will show. The last two chords on the second stave of Example 103a, show an irregular resolution of a German 6th on to the tonic triad of the key of B♭ major (a progression much favoured by César Franck). It will be seen that the augmented 6th (E♮) resolves up a semitone to the dominant (as all well-behaved augmented 6ths do), but the root (G♭), instead of resolving down a semitone to the lower dominant, leaps up a 3rd to the tonic. In fact this is an elision of the standard perfect cadence shown on the stave below these two chords. It functions in the same way as a plagal cadence (chords IV-I, which can be regarded as an elision of the perfect cadence IV-V-I). Now if the augmented 6th is replaced with Berg's near-synonym in bar 227, it will be heard that the effect of this chord resolving on to chord I is almost the same as an augmented 6th resolving in the same way: both are chromatic versions of a plagal cadence. The cadence is heard twice in bars 227-228, but on both occasions the tonic chord is decorated with an added 6th (the whole chord deriving, as we have seen, from notes 7-10 of the prime order).

Instrumentation and texture: Explanations of instrumental abbreviations and performance directions are given in the *Appendix* to the *Anthology*. All of the instruments are notated at sounding pitch. Although the score looks daunting the texture throughout the coda is chamber-like because most of the parts are played by soloists playing at low dynamic levels. When complete sections of strings play in bars 219-222 they delicately double the upper wind with soft pizzicato chords. When they next appear as complete sections (violin 1 and double bass in the last two bars) they play a single melodic line very softly with mutes on.

Berg has labelled the most important melodic lines with the symbols H (*Hauptstimme*, the most important part), N (*Nebenstimme*, the next most important part) and CH (*Choralhauptstimme*, the chorale melody). Thus it is easy to see that in bars 214-219 the most important element in the texture is the two-part counterpoint formed between the chorale melody and the serial solo part (see Example 103b). In the next three bars the horn's *Nebenstimme* reinforces the real bass. The rest of the instruments provide homophonic filling for these important contrapuntal lines. After the high register and narrow range of texture in bars 214-222 the entry of the double bass increases the range to over five octaves. As the strings rise to meet the falling repetitions of the last phrase of the chorale the range narrows again. Then, in the last four bars, the extremes are reached once more with the violin's added 6th sustained in the stratosphere above the root of the chord nearly six octaves below in the double basses.

LAM 110

Britten: Peter Grimes, Act III, Scene 2 (1945)

Title and synopsis: Peter Grimes is a fisherman who is spurned by most of his fellows because they suspect that he is a sadist who allowed his apprentice to die at sea. In the first scene the coroner returns a verdict of accidental death on the boy, but this does not stop the villagers from gossiping. A new apprentice is found. Grimes confesses to Balstrode, one of his few friends, that he intends to *fish the sea dry* in order to earn enough money to marry Ellen Orford, the village schoolmistress. In a monologue, Peter, gazing intently at the sea and an approaching storm, asks *What harbour shelters peace ... away from terrors and tragedies?* (1). His answer is the harbour of Ellen's love *A harbour evermore, Where night is turned to day* (2).

Ellen and Peter go to fetch the new apprentice from a workhouse as the storm gathers strength. The villagers are sheltering in the pub when, at the height of the storm, Ellen, Peter and his apprentice burst in. Ellen consoles the boy: *Goodbye, my dear, God bless you. Peter will take you home* (3). The response of the villagers is unanimous: *Home! do you call that home!.*

On a fine Sunday morning the villagers are at church: Ellen and the apprentice are outside. She is mending his clothes when she discovers that his coat is badly torn and his neck bruised. Peter enters to take the boy fishing. Ellen protests that Sunday should be a day of rest for him. Grimes insists. Ellen mutters *Peter! We've failed!* Peter cries out in agony, strikes Ellen and shouts *So be it, and God have mercy upon me!* (4). When the villagers leave church they hear of this turn of events and accuse Ellen of helping Grimes in his sadistic practices. They set off to hunt Grimes down.

Meanwhile Peter and his apprentice are preparing to go to sea. When chanting villagers approach Peter's hut he hurriedly urges the boy to climb down the cliff. The boy loses his hold and falls to his death. Peter climbs after him and disappears. The villagers inspect the hut and see nothing to alarm them, but Balstrode stays, sees the boy's Sunday clothes and climbs down the way Peter and his apprentice went.

In the first scene of the last act the villagers hear gossip that the boy, who has not been seen for some time, has been murdered by Grimes. Again they set out to find him: this time they intend to lynch him. LAM 110 is taken from the second scene. On the shore in a thick fog the distant cries of the villagers and the mournful sound of a fog-horn can be heard. Peter enters, weary and dementedly singing snatches of melody heard earlier in the opera. Balstrode and Ellen find him. She tries to persuade him to come home, but Balstrode, realising there is no remedy, tells him to go to sea and sink his boat. The next morning the coastguard reports a ship sinking too far out to sea for rescue to be possible. The villagers, believing the report to be an idle rumour, go unconcernedly about their business as the final curtain falls.

Rhythm: Although for convenience the music is barred in 4/4 time, much of it has no regular beat. The frequent pause marks and changes of tempo give only approximate indications of how the demented Grimes is to declaim his recitative (his part is marked *sempre ad lib.* at the start of this scene). Only where close co-ordination between the off-stage chorus and Grimes's monologue is essential does a pulse become briefly apparent (eg *ritmico* in bars 8-10 where Peter's accents fall on strong beats and the chorus' accents fall on weak beats). This lack of a distinct pulse adds to the air of unreality engendered by the fog, the all-but-empty stage and Peter's delirious ravings.

Melody: Peter sings disconnected fragments of melody, some of which are reminiscences of memorable phrases heard in different contexts earlier in the opera. The extract opens with the musical phrase which Britten used at the turning point of the opera, *So be it, and God have mercy upon me* (4 in the third paragraph of the synopsis above). Here the same music is used for his rejection of Ellen's mercy and the villagers' revenge.

The appoggiaturas (E♮s resolving to D♯, the enharmonic equivalent of the fog-horn E♭) in bars 9-11 refer back to the appoggiaturas at the end of Ellen's phrase when she tells the boy that Peter will take him home (3 in the second paragraph of the synopsis above). The mob's motive is a rising semitone in semiquavers (*Peter*) followed by a leap of a minor 3rd to a sustained note (*Grimes*). This is the motive which Peter *roars back to the shouters* at the beginning of bar 12. He distorts it in the following phrases (by free inversion and augmentations of the two intervals of the original motive). Atonal melismas develop on the word *Grimes* until, with the entry of Ellen and Balstrode (bar 14) Peter calms down (musically illustrated by his return to the tonic note of E♭ in bar 15).

Ellen's relatively diatonic phrases (bars 17-21) again refer back to her comforting of Peter's apprentice (3 in paragraph 2 of the synopsis above), thus suggesting that Peter is not much more than a lost child.

The interval of a rising major 9th followed by a diatonic descent is a leitmotiv which runs through the opera as a sign of longing – for love, for peace, for normality. In bars 25-32 it is followed by the same turbulent semiquaver figure (itself derived from the orchestral storm music) which was heard when Peter thought he might find security in Ellen's arms (1 in the first paragraph of the synopsis above). The lyrical extension of the diatonic phrase (bars 33-36) is also a reminiscence of the same scene (2 in the first paragraph of the synopsis above), but now a chromatic descent chokes the dream of peace. Having reached the doom-laden E♭ of the fog-horn Peter falls silent.

Harmony and tonality: The E♭ of the fog horn anchors the often bitonal harmony. In the first three bars, the chorus sustain a chord of E♭ major against the G♭ major tonality of Grimes' phrases (causing an agonising simultaneous false relation on the word *hell*). Grimes' melody in bars 7-11 is in E minor, a tonality which clashes painfully with the women's C major triad, the men's diminished triad on A♮ and the fog-horn E♭. The empty, vindictive-sounding bare 5th on the dominant (bars 12-13) is the backcloth against which Grimes' atonal ravings are heard. In bars 21-27 this bare 5th on the dominant (women) is superimposed on the tonic chord (major and minor) with mournful chromatic appoggiaturas, the last one left unresolved in the bass part of bar 27. In the final bars parallel 5ths (women) and appoggiaturas (men) become ostinati which gradually fade out of earshot leaving just the tonic, E♭, sounding on the fog-horn.

Texture: Britten is famous for the startling effects he achieves with the utmost economy of means. In this passage the only instrument is an off-stage tuba playing just two pitches, yet fulfilling three functions:

1) it effectively mimics a fog-horn with the baleful drop in pitch that is heard momentarily when the wind pressure stops,

2) the interval of a minor 2nd reflects and is reflected by the semitonal motive: notice particularly the way Peter's last two notes and the basses' last appoggiatura (F♭-E♭) is echoed by the tuba (E♭-D♮) in the last three bars,

3) it provides a tonal anchor for the unaccompanied voices (both a practical point of reference for pitching and a structural unifying device).

The unaccompanied off-stage chorus varies from two-part male-voice monotones answering each other like baying hounds (bars 5-6), through four-part female homophony (bars 1-3) and six-part antiphony (bars 8-11) to a vibrant tutti chord at the extreme upper registers of the voices (bar 12). The simplicity of these off-stage parts allows the audience to focus its attention on the pathetic ravings of Grimes (who needs to be played by a consummate actor-musician).

English had never become an established genre (Handel's operas, eg LAM 26, were Italian both stylistically and textually). With *Peter Grimes* Britten established opera in English as a genre which was respected throughout the world. It paved the way for his own later operas and for those of his compatriots such as Tippett and Harrison Birtwistle.

LAM 111

Stockhausen: Kontra-Punkte, 1st Movement (1953)

Title: The title is an elaborate pun. It means "counterpoint" in the traditional sense, but written as two hyphenated words it also means "against points", meaning that it is a rejection of the pointillist textures of his earlier composition, *Punkte* in particular, and of earlier modernist music such as Webern's *Quartet* Op.22 (LAM 100) in general. This interpretation of the title makes no sense when one looks at the tiny extract given in the *Anthology* (which is even more pointillist in texture than the Webern *Quartet*). One needs to know that the whole work involves the gradual elimination of each instrument in turn until only one timbre is left, that of the piano. Thus it moves from the many-coloured pointillist texture of the opening to the monochrome colour and two-part counterpoint of the piano alone.

Rhythm: As with most avant-garde works of the 50s and 60s no pulse can be detected (the barring in 3/8 time is for the convenience of the performers). The extreme complexity of the rhythms produces a series of sound-events, the articulation of which appears to be quite random. Similarly, although durations are precisely notated (with the exception of two bassoon notes and one trombone note), the aural effect is quite random. This is because such a variety of durations are used, ranging from less than a demisemiquaver to six quavers' length. Furthermore the lengths are often of great complexity in relation to the quaver unit of time (2.833333 quavers in one case!).

Melody: In the extract a number of cells emerge from bar 8 onwards, each of them confined to one instrument and hence identifiable by the timbre of the instrument. They are all extremely angular, the intervals used being dissonant (minor 9ths, major 7ths and a tritone) or comprising compound consonances (compound perfect 4ths and compound major 3rds). There is no attempt here (or, indeed, in the whole work) to develop these motives in the traditional manner.

Harmony: When two or more notes sound together the combination is always dissonant (with the sole exception of the perfect 4th at the start). As with the melodic cells there is no attempt here or in the rest of the work to develop these aggregations of pitches.

Texture and timbre: These are the most important parameters of the aural phenomena. The work is scored for a chamber ensemble of ten soloists which Stockhausen thought of as being grouped into six timbral entities: three groups of winds (flute and bassoon, clarinet and bass clarinet, trumpet and trombone), one group of bowed strings (violin and cello), one group of plucked strings (harp), and one group of hammered strings (piano) – the wide ranges of the last two entitling them to be regarded as discrete groups. Elsewhere in *Kontra-Punkte* the pairs of melody instruments work together, but in the extract this is not apparent.

Every note or cell is given one of six dynamic levels ranging from *ppp* to *f*. Within these dynamic levels further nuances are indicated by hairpins and accents. The range of instrumental colour is tremendous and is affected by the dynamic marks. There are ten timbres corresponding with the ten solo instruments, but these tone colours are modified by the use of mutes on the brass instruments, the use of muted and unmuted strings, and the use of the fingertip or fingernail in the middle of the string and near the pinboard on the harp (a most subtle colouristic effect is produced by playing enharmonics on two strings using different plucking techniques in bar 5). Since timbre is necessarily affected by dynamic level, there are almost as many timbres as there are notes in this extract.

There are seven points at which two or more notes are articulated simultaneously to produce a chord. No two of these involve the same instrumental combinations:

Bar 1: clarinet *(mp)* and harp *(p)*,
Bar 6: clarinet *(mf)*, trumpet *(p dim.)* and cello *(pp dim)*,
Bar 7: bassoon *(p)*, violin *(f dim.)* and cello *(f cresc.)*,

Bar 8[1]: flute *(ppp)* and bassoon *(p)*
Bar 8[3]: 2 harp notes differentiated by playing technique *(mp)*,
Bar 12: trombone *(pp cresc.)* and piano *(mf)*,
Bar 15: bassoon *(f)* and cello *(mp cres.)*.

At other points two or more differently-pitched timbres combine as a result of the overlapping of separately articulated notes: there are too many to describe in detail. At only one point is the same pitch articulated simultaneously by different instruments (bassoon and trombone in bar 4).

The effect of the wide variety of texture and timbre is to produce what Stockhausen described as "maximum scatter" (which progresses to maximum coherence as the work unfolds).

Compositional technique: All 12 chromatic degrees are heard once only in the first five bars. This might lead one to expect the use of serial technique in the rest of the work. If this is the case it is unclear how Stockhausen has manipulated his row in the rest of this extract. Nor does there appear to be a predetermined ordering of the parameters of duration and dynamics.

LAM 112

Boulez: Le Marteau sans Maître: IX (1955)

Title, text and context: The title of the music is also the title of a collection of surrealist poems by René Char, written in 1934 and first published in 1945. Literally translated it means "The Hammer without a master". From them Boulez chose three poems to be sung by a contralto. Each of these songs is connected with one or two instrumental commentaries in which music takes over from text as the principal focus of attention. The extract is taken from the end of the ninth and last movement, *Bel édifice et les pressentiments – double* (Variation upon "Beautiful building and premonitions"). This is the title of the poem which Boulez set in the fifth movement. It consists of surreal images of a "dead sea" the waves of which wash over the poets head, and of "pure eyes in the woods" which weep as they "seek the head to live in". These are dream-images like Salvador Dali's melting watches. Whatever meaning they have is that which the individual reader cares to ascribe to them. Similarly with the wondrous sounds that Boulez conjures from thin air: the significance (if any) is that which the listener allows to be evoked by his perception of the changing textures and timbres of the music.

Bel édifice is more than a simple variation of the fifth movement. It is a coda to the whole cycle in that references are made to the other movements as well. LAM 112, the last 51 bars of the last movement, refers back to the vocal melismas of the third movement, a setting of "Furious artisans" for voice and flute. In this "commentary" the flute takes over the vocal melismas of the original, while the singer (with her mouth closed) is reduced to the role of a subsidiary instrument. Eventually even the flute disappears in the haze of the dying sound of a suspended cymbal.

Rhythm: The rhythms are of such complexity that it is impossible to detect a pulse. This is not surprising since the notated metres change 45 times, and the tempi nine times (with intermediate accelerandi and ritardani) in the space of 51 bars. Not only are individual notes more often articulated off the beat than on, but mathematically irrational ratios of long to short notes are common. The flautist is also required to add grace notes of no defined duration. Often several of these rhythmic parameters coincide. For instance in bar 154 the flute enters at a change of metre, places a grace note before a note lasting three semiquavers and another lasting two semiquavers, both of them to be played in the time of a group of four semiquavers (conducted as two quavers) whilst speeding up from 56 crotchets per minute to 63 crotchets per minute in the next bar. All of this is, of course, carefully calculated to produce an improvisatory effect whilst synchronising the soloist's arabesques with the accompanying instruments.

Melody: Atonal and extremely angular. Boulez wrote that he composed *Le Marteau* at a time "when strict serialism was being abandoned in the hope of discovering more general and more flexible laws governing sound phenomena". Dodecaphonic series are presented in *Le Marteau*, but they are not apparent in this extract.

Harmony: Chords are dissonant by-products of the coincidence of contrapuntal lines.

Texture: This varies from the polyphony of bars 153-154 (maximum textural density), through the pointillism of bars 144-146 (intermediate density), to the monophony of bars 164-188 (minimum density).

Timbre: Along with rhythm this is probably the most important parameter of the music. Boulez chose the alto flute (Fl. en sol) because its range (a 4th lower than the usual flute in C) and timbral quality corresponds better with the range and timbre of the contralto soloist than its smaller brother. Two special effects are required of the flautist: flutter-tonguing (eg bar 157), and the peculiar sound produced by audibly hitting the key simultaneously with the articulation of the note (bar 186).

The xylorimba was similarly chosen because it has more lower notes than the xylophone, so it too matches the lower range of the contralto voice. Likewise he chose a viola rather than a violin or cello.

Two other factors determined the choice of instruments. Firstly Boulez wished not only to contrast the timbres, he also hoped that the listener would notice how they complemented each other in couples. Thus the voice and flute both rely on breath as the instigator of tone. The flute and viola are both monodic instruments. The viola when played pizzicato (eg bar 144) and the guitar are both plucked string instruments. The vibraphone and xylorimba are both struck.

Secondly he wished the listener to make connections between certain instruments and their non-European counterparts. He likened the xylorimba to the African balafrom, the vibraphone to the Balinese gender (see LAM 97) and the guitar to the Japanese koto.

LAM 117

Lennon and McCartney: Eleanor Rigby (1967)

Title and text: A ballad about the loneliness, futility and death of a spinster, and the equally meaningless life of the priest who buries her. There is compassion, but also despair: no one was saved in this life or the next (if there is one). The verse form is simple, but it conveys the message with clarity and precision:

Introduction:

Ah, look at all the lonely people!	5 feet (repeat)

Verse:

Eleanor Rigby picks up the rice	4 feet, A
In the church where a wedding has been,	3 feet, B
Lives in a dream.	2 feet, B (repeat)

Refrain:

All the lonely people,	3 feet
Where do they all come from?	3 feet
All the lonely people,	3 feet
Where do they all belong?	3 feet

ABB = the rhyme scheme of the verses (the introduction and refrain are unrhymed). The use of lines in which the number of metrical feet reduces by one each time and the use of rhyme at the end of the verse highlights the importance of the last line of each stanza (*Lives in a dream, Who is it for?, No-one comes near, What does he care, Nobody came, No-one was saved*). The lack of rhyme in the refrain is compensated by the regularity of the metrical scheme.

Melody and form: The textual accents fall either on the first beat of a bar or are syncopated. At no point does a verbal or musical accent fall on any other beat of the bar (not even on the nominally strong third beat). The syncopated articulation of a note/syllable just before the beat (a push) strengthens rather than weakens the verbal accent (eg *lone, peo, do, from* in the refrain). Accents on the first beat of a bar define the phrase structure of the melody which is subtly at variance with the versification:

Introduction:
3-bar vocal phrase + 1 bar instrumental fill (repeated)
Verse:
5 bars phrased 1 + 3 + 1 (repeated)
Chorus:
4 + 4

Disregarding the introduction, the overall form is:
Verse:
A (bars 5-9), A (bars 10-14)
Chorus:
B (bars 15-18), B^1 (bars 19-22)

This pattern is strophically repeated (the words of A change, the words of B and B^1 remain constant). The one-bar phrases at the start each verse (bars 5 and 10) divide the names of the lonely people (Eleanor Rigby and Father McKenzie) from the rest of the first line of the text. The three-bar phrases (bars 6-8 and 11-13) run straight through from this point in the first line of the text to the end of the next line (helped by a sequential descent from D♮ to A♮). The long note on the last syllable of the three-bar phrases further emphasises the detachment of them from the one-bar phrases/two-foot lines (bars 9 and 14). In the chorus B^1 differs from B in two significant ways. The leap of an octave in B is augmented to become a much more impassioned leap of a 10th in B^1. B ends as expected on the tonic note (E♮), but B^1 ends the chorus and the song on a much less conclusive G♮ (the mediant), the tonal uncertainty of which reflects the unanswered question, *Where do they all belong?*.

As with many Beatles' songs the melody is modal, in this case the Dorian mode transposed to E. The most characteristic feature of this mode is the sharpened 6th degree (C♯) and the flattened 7th degree (D♮). Both are heard prominently in bars 6 and 11. Up to bar 8 the 6th and 7th degrees of the scale have either been avoided or have been part of the Dorian mode. So when a C♮ appears in bars 9 and 14 it sounds chromatic and dissonant (it clashes with the B in the E minor chord which accompanies it). This again highlights the detached one-bar phrase/two-foot line, the importance of which has already been emphasised.

Harmony and tonality: The accompaniment is remarkable for its use of only two chords, an E minor triad on the first degree of the Dorian mode on E, and a C major triad on the sixth degree (both in root position). At no point is the sharpened 7th heard, so, in the absence of this D♯ these two chords remain entirely modal. There is, however, tension between the sharpened 6th degree of the Dorian mode in the melody and the flattened 6th degree upon which the C major triad rests. This tension is reflected in the chromatic descent in the string accompaniment of the chorus (D♮, C♯, C♮ and B in bars 15-18, repeated in the next four bars).

LAM 119

Tavener: Ultimos Ritos: 5th Movement (1972)

Historical context: Tavener first attracted widespread attention with his dramatic cantata *The Whale*. So successful was this in "The Swinging 60s" that the Beatles (LAM 117) arranged for it to be recorded on their Apple label.

Tavener's style is eclectic and runs directly counter to the modernism of composers such as Stockhausen (LAM 111) and Boulez (LAM 112). Where Stockhausen and Boulez relish displays of intellectual brilliance, Tavener attempts to entice his audience with mystical contemplation. Where the modernists engage the mind, Tavener engages the spirit. It is strange that Messiaen should have been such a seminal influence for both camps: his *Mode de valeurs et d'intensités* influencing the integral serialism of the one, and his mystical, intense harmony of stasis the other (or perhaps this just shows how catholic Messiaen was in both his music and his spirituality). A comparison of the methods of Boulez and Stockhausen on the one hand and Tavener on the other with Messiaen's *Quatuor pour la fin du temps* (LAM 108) will reveal the intellectual control of the former (in the use of strictly regulated modes of pitch and rhythm), and the sensuality/spirituality of the latter (in the use of non-functional chromatic harmony). Could it be said that the spirit of Messiaen lives on in the mysticism of

Title and texts: *Ultimos Ritos* = Last Rites. Tavener here combines the Latin text of that passage of the *Credo* (an affirmation of Christian belief) which deals with the crucifixion with Verses written upon an ecstasy by the Spanish mystic, St. John of the Cross. The text of the *Credo* appears in two forms:

1) A pre-recorded performance of sections of Bach's *Mass in B minor*. These are shown on the lowest ten staves of pages 412 and 413. They are superimposed on the live performance. The text at this point translates as "He was crucified for us ...".

2) Sung live by four choruses with the syllables divided between them – *sub* (choir 3, bar 204) *Pon* (choir 4, bar 206) *ti* (choir 3, bar 210) *o* (choir 2, bar 213) *Pi* (choir 1, bar 216) *la* (choir 2, bar 220) *to* (choir 3, bar 222) *pas* (choir 4, bar 223) *sus* (choir 3, bar 230) *et* (choir 2, bar 235 – *est* is probably a misprint in the full score). The text at this point (*sub Pontio Pilato, passus et ...*) translates as a continuation of "He was crucified for us ... under Ponius Pilate, he suffered and (was buried)".

The text of St. John's verses are also distributed, this time amongst the four soloists – *si* (tenor, bar 201) *lo que* (soprano, bar 206 and 212) *reis* (tenor, bar 218) *o* (soprano, bar 220) *ir* (alto, bar 225) *Consis* (soprano, bar 227 and 231) *te es* (tenor, bar 231 and 234). The text at this point (*si lo quereis oir, consiste es*) is shown in full in the *Appendix*.

Harmony: There are three levels of harmony:

A) Four-part non-functional harmony shown in the top two staves of Example 119 (all four choirs sing the same chords). Disregarding the tenor solo (TS) D♯ and the alto solo (AS) G♯, the chords are those which could have been used by any late 19th century composer, but not juxtaposed in this particular progression. They are:

    1) a C major triad in first inversion with a major 7th (B♮) above the root,

    2) a half-diminished 7th in root position, first inversion and third inversion,

    3) a dominant 7th in third inversion.

B) Internal pedals sung by the soloists. In Example 119 the tenor soloist's D is dissonant with chords 1 and 2, the alto soloist's G♯ is consonant with chord 2 but adds a major 13th to the dominant 7th chord (3).

C) Bach's chromatic but functional harmony is in E minor. In this respect it differs radically from Tavener's non-functional harmony, but some of the parts coincide, notably the E minor chord at the start of Example 119, and the dominant on B♮ at the end.

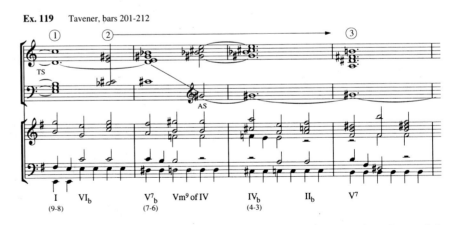

Ex. 119   Tavener, bars 201-212

Texture: The polychoral effect of the four four-part choruses is enhanced by spatial separation (the performers are distributed to form the shape of a cross). In this passage they differ from one another only by their separated delivery of the syllables of the *Credo*. More intimately the soloists declaim an extended monodic line carrying the verses of St John of the Cross. The tape of Bach's setting of the *Crucifixus* is divided into seven four-bar phrases which are superimposed on the live singers. The seventh of these phrases buries Tavener's own composition: the intention being that it should represent the abnegation of the self in willing obedience to God's will (just as Christ himself surrendered his life for mankind).